THE ART OF
WRIST-SPIN BOWLING

THE ART OF
Wrist-Spin Bowling

PETER PHILPOTT

The Crowood Press

First published in 1995 by
The Crowood Press Ltd
Ramsbury, Marlborough
Wiltshire SN8 2HR

Paperback edition 1997

This impression 2002

British Library Cataloguing-in-Publication Data
A catalogue record for this book is available from the British Library.

ISBN 1 86126 063 6

Picture credits
All line drawings by Tom Briggs

Throughout this book, 'he', 'him' and 'his' have been used as neutral
pronouns and as such refer to both males and females.

Typeset by Intype, London

Printed and bound in Great Britain by Bookcraft, Midsomer Norton

Contents

Acknowledgements

My thanks go to those who supplied photographs, especially Patrick Eagar and Jeffrey Walker, and to Tom Briggs for other illustrations; to C.B. Naish for the use of his work in *The Physics of Ball Games*; to the Rossall School for the help of the boys and use of the facilities; to my wife, Judy, for her frequent advice and her work on the word processor, without which this book would never have materialized.

Keith Andrew and Brian Taber were both fine wicket-keepers, which makes them honorary members of the Wrist-Spinner's Club. Keith played with Northamptonshire and England, and Brian with New South Wales and Australia. After outstanding playing careers, both became Directors of Coaching for their respective countries. They held these important positions during decades when so much in the cricket coaching world was revolutionized and made permanent contributions to the game. I am grateful and flattered by their eagerness to write the forewords. I thank them both and hope they enjoy this book.

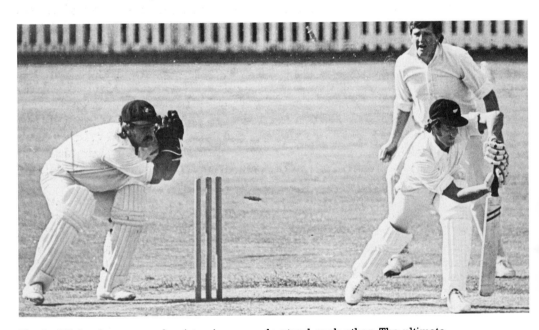

Fig 1 Wicket-keepers and wrist-spinners understand each other. The ultimate for both is a stumping when the bowlers' skill defeats the batsman. Here Rod Marsh takes them off with Keith Stackpole watching, but Dayle Hadlee retains his balance and his wicket.

Forewords

This unique and long-overdue book could only have been written by one man, Peter Philpott – Australian Test cricketer, dedicated teacher and world-class cricket coach. Like many Australian cricketers, Peter is the total enthusiast, a modest man, not an uncommon trait amongst the truly talented. His record speaks for him. Of course he is fortunate in coming from a long line of Australian wrist-spin bowlers: Clarrie Grimmett, Bill O'Reilly, Fleetwood Smith, Cec Pepper, George Tribe, Bruce Dooland and Richie Benaud to name but a few of the very best. Today we have the amazing Shane Warne, a product of Australia's policy in developing spin bowling talent and a young man who could surpass them all. Peter Philpott's twenty years of specialized coaching, particularly of Australia's elite young spinner looks to have been a wonderful investment.

As a young wicketkeeper playing in the Central Lancashire League, a second home to many fine overseas cricketers, I was lucky to keep wicket to George Tribe, a magnificent left-arm wrist-spinner from Victoria. Later we became team-mates for Northamptonshire CCC in the mid-fifties. It was this experience that gave me a lifelong enthusiasm for the art and craft of wrist-spin bowling and probably qualified me to write this foreword. Perhaps I am biased, but wicket-keepers do have the advantage of seeing the whole of the wrist-spinner's performance and not just the first act, which is the lot of most batsmen.

Apart from the variety that spin-bowling introduces into the game, it makes such a contribution to the spectacle as a whole – more overs bowled, more runs scored, less negative play and a lot more fun for player and spectator. I am pleased to know that Mickey Stewart my friend and colleague of many years and now England's Director of Coaching is to work with Peter on a coaching film to go with this book. I suspect both will be bestsellers and a revelation to cricketers young and old everywhere.

Keith Andrew
England and Northamptonshire CCC
Former Chief Executive, National
Cricket Association
June, 1994

It is with great pleasure that I write this foreword. I have been fortunate to have played with and against Peter on many occasions, both in club and first-class cricket. He had a fine personal career with the bat and ball, and enjoyed the game more than most.

From playing days we have developed a close relationship in the coaching area. Peter has made major contributions to the Australian Cricket Board Advanced Course coaching since its inception in 1973. His knowledge of the game has enabled him to lecture/present on all aspects of the game.

In addition to his knowledge, however, is an outstanding ability to communicate and teach at all levels from the youngsters at school to the Test match players. Peter has been a teacher most of his life, but has also been Coach of New South Wales and South Australian Sheffield Shield teams, and the first Australian team coach to tour England.

I am pleased to see him go to print on his first love, 'wrist-spin bowling'. Most of us are delighted to see the wrist-spinner making his mark on the game, as Shane Warne is. If Peter's work can continue to encourage more participation and involvement for spinners then cricket will be the winner.

I shall look forward to reading the book, and I am sure that all cricketers, spinners or not, will enjoy it. I wish him well with the book and hope that, from the readers of its contents we might obtain another player of Peter's ability and attitude.

Brian Taber
National Director of Coaching,
Australia
August, 1994

CHAPTER 1

Oh, for Some Spin Again

Cricket history bubbles over with the humour of spin bowlers. They have been the jovial men of the game.

From all accounts, Arthur Mailey must have been the foremost comedian of his era, not excluding the nimble-footed Charles Chaplin. In more recent times, and closer to my own experience, it has been the slow bowlers and wicket-keepers who have supplied the majority of cricket's light-hearted moments. I include wicket-keepers because all of them are spin bowlers at heart.

A normal conversation between Johnny Martin and Wally Grout would have been a smash hit on any vaudeville stage. To be in the company of Norm O'Neill (also a member of the leg-spin club) and Barry Jarman for any length of time was inviting a heart attack from non-stop laughter. To play with, and listen to, the wit of Cecil Pepper and Jack Pettiford was to add an entirely new dimension to the art of repartee. Somehow, spinning a yarn goes hand in hand with the spinning of a ball; the ability to put on a turn and bounce at a social gathering carries over into a man's bowling.

I suppose a sense of humour is essential for the slow bowler. How else could he retain sanity on the 'bad days'? Those days when the sixes not only clear the oval boundaries but the

municipal boundaries as well. Those days when his follow through after delivery becomes a quick-footed retreat behind the umpire as hungry batsmen stampede down the wicket to get at him. Those days when his only value to the fielding side is the possibility of run-outs as batsmen crucify each other trying to get to the striker's end. Let's face it, for slow bowlers it is either laugh or cry – and by the time he has reached first-class cricket there are no tears left.

Nor are tears associated with medium-paced bowlers. For these are the solemn, poker-faced men of the game, humourless, dour, uncompromising. They are the bank managers of cricket who wish to save and play safe – at any cost. Certainly they give nothing away, preferring the safety of containment than the speculation of buying wickets.

The spinner is inflationary, but the medium-pacer follows deflationary policies to the point of depression. Can you picture a Trevor Bailey or a Slasher Mackay at work in the cricket field in any other way but this sombre humourless role?

No, the medium-pacers cannot join the slow bowlers in mirth. Indeed, the very operation of a spinner during a match, as he spins, flights and tempts, usually brings a frown to the already serious countenance of the seamer. The spinner's rapid over-rate and lack of thrift disturb and alarm him. Nor are the pacemen renowned for their sunny dispositions. True they do raise a half-smile at times and have been known to snigger through grated teeth. A middle stump cart-wheeling, a batsman reeling to the pitch when avoiding a screaming bouncer, the sickening thump of leather on ribs, the white-faced young batsman cringing back towards square-leg – these are the catalysts of fast-bowling humour. These galloping ghouls are a sadistic bunch and glory in it.

So it seems, that among the bowling fraternity humour flourishes with the spinners alone.

Alas, today the game has fallen, literally, into the hands of pace and seam. Cricket has become an assault featuring ducking, bobbing and weaving, long run-ups, slow over-rates, fierce glances and solemn batsmen deflecting from a back-foot commitment. It has become a contest of physical strength varied only by the temporary appearance of some long-faced medium-pacer who doggedly wastes time while his stronger and more ruthless brethren take a breather and contemplate their next fierce frontal assault.

And with the departure of the spinners, the humour has gone. The increase of on-field bickering – of 'sledging', as it is now called – is no surprise under the circumstances. There is not much left for batsmen to smile about, and any slow bowler continuing to exist amidst this wilderness of brute strength must find little joy in the atmosphere. The thinning and

Fig 2   Lance Gibbs gave the ball an almighty flick – and is thereby admitted to the Wrist-Spinners' Club.

greying of Lance Gibb's hair may not have been the product of age but rather of his solitary confinement as a spinner in modern cricket.

Will the spinners return? Can we look forward again to the dazzling, twinkle-toed footwork of attacking batsmanship; the diving, active work of fieldsmen in front of the wicket; the full-blooded straight driven six hits; the sleight-of-hand skill of stumping; the guile of googly and top-spinner; the joy of cricket when bowlers connive to get batsmen out and batsmen set out to destroy bowlers? Or is cricket forever condemned to the present war of attrition which so many of us find deadly dull and monotonous?

I began to write this piece with tongue in cheek. It was the whimsy of an ex-spinner. But, as I considered the possibility of pace and seam dominating the old game into eternity (*ad nauseam*, you might say), my thoughts became serious, then morbid and forlorn. For cricket must have spin to balance the game.

Doubtless, the opening over of a Test match is the high point of tension and excitement. The sight of Wes Hall in full fury was awe-inspiring. The skill and rhythm of Ray Lindwall and Dennis Lillee in action were a joy to watch for any cricketer. And all of us could appreciate the power and pace of Jeff Thomson.

Grant all this – but, oh, for some spin again!

I wrote the above article, 'Oh, for Some Spin Again' in 1976 for the *Australian Cricket Magazine*. As I said, it did begin tongue-in-cheek, and it did become serious as it progressed. For by 1976, I had been actively 'spreading the word' for wrist-spin wherever I could for almost twenty years. This was in many parts of the cricketing world, but particularly, in New South Wales and Australia generally. It was because I had been brought up in a cricketing philosophy which demanded wrist-spin as an integral part of the game, because I so enjoyed being part of the wrist-spin fraternity and understood what an absorbing art it was, and because, by the late 1960s, I detected a change in attitude which disturbed me. This was the apparent

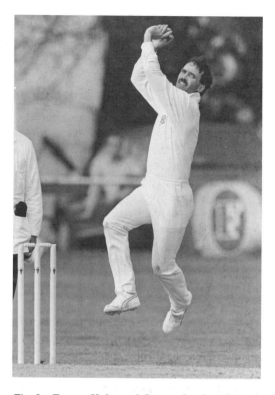

Fig 3   Trevor Hohns of Queensland and Australia moves rhythmically into his delivery position. Note the left hand still disguising his right hand grip. (Patrick Eagar)

loss of faith in wrist-spin in a modern cricket obsessed by containment.

Those early years of coaching wrist-spin for the interest of many enthusiasts, became, in the seventies an increasingly worried and frustrated campaign to help save it from total extinction. The drift away of the early seventies became rapids by the late seventies and a precipitous waterfall of apparent no-return by the eighties. Indeed, by the early to mid-eighties, many of my colleagues had accepted, whilst I had at least feared, that the

Fig 4   Bob Holland came into first-class cricket quite late in his career for New South Wales and Australia. See how much of a flick he has given this leg-spinner.

skill of wrist-spin was finished in modern cricket.

Certainly, individuals appeared on occasions to keep the thought alive – though hardly kicking. These exceptions, such as Terry Jenner, Kerry O'Keefe, Jim Higgs, Bob Holland and Trevor Hohns disproved the apparent rule that wrist-spin was no longer required, but the fact remained that in most parts of the cricketing world, it had all but been forgotten – not only its skills, but its traditions, philosophies and very *raison d'etre*. Play-

ers and captains no longer understood it or how it should be handled, and misunderstanding, as so often happens, became suspicion and then, eventually, dislike.

I was particularly depressed when I discovered that even Sri Lanka had discarded spin as a serious attacking weapon in Test cricket. This discovery was made when I visited Colombo to work with the Sri Lankan national team before its visits to Australia in 1983 and 1985. Local authorities argued that English opinion had convinced them that only pace and seam had a future in success at Test level. Spin at that level, they said seriously, was a thing of the past.

In the short term there was little point in arguing, as few spinners were available or considered for those tours of Australia. Little wonder with such official thinking. But I thought back to the two spinners who had almost skittled Australia in the 1981 visit en route to England. It was the off-spinner and left-arm spinner, in combination, who had bamboozled the Australian batsmen on turning wickets, not the quicks.

Furthermore I looked around at the physical conditions of Sri Lanka. First the climate, which is not friendly towards pace; second the wickets, which are more conducive to spin; and third the physique of most Sri Lankans who have the physical attributes of spin bowlers rather than pace bowlers. If ever a country should concentrate on the skills and traditions of spin of all types, it is surely Sri Lanka. Yet the generalized opinion of some outsider, foreign to their conditions, had received a blanket acceptance, it seemed. A long tradition had been cast aside because of a search for theoretical types in a country unsuited for and unnatural to such types.

It was most depressing. If Sri Lanka had discarded all spin, let alone wrist-spin, what did the future hold. It left me frustrated and most disturbed about the future course of cricket everywhere.

Abdul Qadir, during this period, was like a beacon signalling to all, that talented leg-spinning remained a unique and major attacking weapon in any age. But it was a beacon ignored by most, whom, I believe were sailing the beautiful yacht of cricket onto the reefs.

Of course, I was not the only one to feel so strongly – to believe that a cricket dominated by medium-pace containment, or a barrage of rib-height, short-of-a-length pace bowled at funereal over-rates created a game both unattractive and unbalanced. Many of us believed that spin – and wrist-spin in particular – was desperately needed back in the game for many reasons.

My own coaching work was not going to change matters alone. But if it won any support from players, administrators, or lovers of the game, it was worth it. It might at least maintain a memory.

By the mid-eighties in Australia, the spin-coaching clinics I had been conducting for so long in various States of Australia were accepted officially by the Australian Cricket Board and developed into a coordinated Australia-wide spin coaching programme. It became the 'Spin Australia' programme, in the fingers and hands of Ashley Mallett and myself. And, around that point of time, with a deep, but carefully contained excitement, I thought I began to notice a change at last. Not only were some youngsters with leg-spin talent beginning to appear and a general renewal of interest suggesting itself, but it was made clear that selectors at the top in Australia – Test and some State – were seeking and wanting wrist-spin talent.

Australian cricket – and perhaps world cricket as a whole – probably owes a great deal to Lawry Sawle, John Benaud, Jim Higgs and Bob Simpson, the Australian Selection Committee of the early 1990s, for that decision and commitment alone. Wrist-spin was back in vogue.

The selection of both Peter McIntyre and Shane Warne for an Australian B Tour of Zimbabwe further emphasized this commitment. Neither had been favoured by their own State selectors at the time, neither had the necessary performance qualification, but the Australian selectors put their money where their mouths were.

With such official interest and encouragement there began a noticeable revival of wrist-spin in schools and beyond. Not that it was a return to the 1950s or earlier, but, at least, 'wristies' were sought, chosen and bowled reasonably when they deserved to. We were on the way again.

The 1993 series between England and Australia was a culmination of this growing movement. The performance of Shane Warne on that tour did more for wrist-spinning than any thirty odd years of coaching could have done.

Fig 5   Tim May is a world-class off-spinner who really gives the ball a flick. A beautiful body position here, but note the position of the back foot. It indicates the huge body rotation about to help his spin and 'oomph'. It also indicates the need for great flexibility and tough knees. (Patrick Eagar)

Fig 6   Shane Warne. Sheer poetry in the total relaxation, fluency and rhythm. Every detail of the action is perfection. (Patrick Eagar)

Shane bowled superbly (aided by some appalling English batting) though no better than off-spinner, Tim May.

But Warne captured the public imagination. The youth, vitality and charisma of the thick-set, ear-ringed blond had the ingredients of a pop star idol in an era of unprecedented TV coverage. His first ball in English Test cricket, with its drift, drop and prodigious turn, mesmerized the experienced Mike Gatting and won the awe, respect and imagination of a huge audience. Warne has immense talent and potential; he should be a great international bowler eventually; but he owes a great deal to the power of modern media.

I arrived in England towards the end of that series, but immediately became aware of the depth of public imagination that Warne had captured. A renewed interest in the all but forgotten art was apparent, in my opinion, and that opinion was confirmed when Mickey Stewart almost immediately invited me to speak on wrist-spin to a seminar of TCCB coaches at Lilleshall Hall in October 1993. The warmth of my reception and the discussions which ensued there amongst that experienced and expert audience confirmed my belief that the demand for the return of wrist-spin to the old game was world-wide and strong. How sensible at last!

At Lilleshall, many enthusiastic coaches insisted that I should produce a book on leg-spin. I was fully aware that expertise in this field in Australia was very thin, the same seemed to be so in England, and was likely to be similar world-wide. Having published several coaching books previously, I had often considered one solely devoted to wrist-spin. It was an exciting and attractive challenge.

In November, whilst in London, I visited Lords to meet an old cricketing acquaintance and colleague, Keith Andrew. Keith had been a wicket-keeper for Northamptonshire and England. He joined the National Cricket Association in 1975, had been Director of Coaching since 1979, and Chief Executive of the NCA since 1986. He had devoted most of his life to cricket and coaching in particular.

It is no exaggeration to say that this book was to a very great extent motivated by Keith's enthusiasm and I thank him for it. It was he who argued that a book had to be written and that to the skills and techniques should be added something which attempted to convey the ethos, the traditions and the philosophy which has made, and always will make, wrist-spinning something special.

Wrist-spin bowling has made up a very large slab of my life since the age of six – not only through a long playing career, but also through an equally long coaching career. All that time, I have believed totally in the importance of wrist-spin as an integral component of attacking cricket and a balanced game.

I am quite confident that my belief in the importance of wrist-spin is sound, that my knowledge of it is deep and wide, and that my love for it remains untarnished. Thus if this book enables me to pass on just a small part of that knowledge, commitment and enthusiasm, I shall be more than satisfied.

CHAPTER 2

Some Ground Rules

Let's get things straight from the outset. This book is about *spin* bowling – not slow bowling, but spin bowling. What makes spin bowling different from other forms of bowling is, so obviously, the spin. And spin and spinning the ball are the core of the matter. This seems unarguable – *cela va sans dire*, as my old French teacher used to say. But, apparently, it is not. For, too often, discussion of spin bowling focuses on the grip, accuracy, delivery, field placement, tactics, but says very little about spin itself.

I intend to start with spin and continue to emphasize spin throughout this book. That does not mean that I ignore the importance of accuracy. Of course, it is essential. But spin bowling is what we are talking about and so spin comes first.

In particular this book concentrates on *wrist-spin*. That is an unfortunate description because it implies that only the wrist is used in the action. Yet, to bowl wrist-spin with real spin requires not only the wrist, but all the fingers, the forearm, the elbow, the shoulder, both arms, the entire body and the total bowling action. Naturally I shall elaborate on this later. The other misfortune of the term, 'wrist-spin', is the implication that its brother, 'finger-spin', is based on fingers alone with no involvement of

the wrist. If that is so – and it is with some bowlers – it is ineffective. For the finger-spinner who really wishes to spin the ball requires all of the same ingredients as the wrist-spinner. So, though most readers will understand what the term 'wrist-spin' implies, I shall define my points of reference clearly now.

This book is about leg-spin bowled by right-hand bowlers, and off-spin bowled by left-hand bowlers.

You can call them wrist-spinners, 'wristies', 'leggies', 'chinamen', or whatever you wish, but from hereon in the game plan is clear. And always the emphasis will be on spin and getting batsmen out rather than line and length, containment, and boring batsmen out.

With such criteria clarified, it is almost time to go on. But, first, some more clarifications. There will be times in this book when I repeat myself. That should be no real worry, as there is a repetitive element in the acquisition of any skill. But it is probably more so in this particular book because of the way in which I have approached it. I have concentrated on spin first and foremost, describing and explaining the skills and drills to achieve it. These skills are dealt with

Fig 7 Johnny Martin. An exciting little cricketer who could bowl spells of penetrative left-arm wrist-spin – a Chinaman.

meant to be exact age divisions, such as Stage One is for age groups six to eight, and so on. Certainly a six-year-old could begin to approach Stage One, and, as soon as he is ready, go on to Stage Two. But Stage One will never be finished, and he should always go back to these early stages at some time, even if he reaches the very top of the game.

Further, bowlers may come to this book long after the age of six. Many a cricketer has eventually 'seen the light', and has come to wrist-spinning quite late in his career. He too, should begin at Stage One and progress at his own pace. One warning for such a

Fig 8 Here is 'another one' just starting. The release of his leg-break.

in stages, all of which overlap to a certain extent. Moreover, some of the spin skills are closely inter-related to others, such as those associated with the attainment of accuracy or certain variations. Thus, repetition is inevitable. I simply wish you to know that I am aware of it, and believe that, if anything, such repetition is advantageous.

When 'stages' are used, they are not

late-comer. Just because you are older, it does not follow that you will, or can, conquer each stage more quickly than a youngster. Alas, it may well take you longer.

Children can begin to learn any skill at almost any age. Never under-rate them. Their in-built computer is as efficient as an adult's, it has simply been fed less information as yet. Of course, what information is fed in at what age requires sympathetic judge-ment. But the fact is that often a youngster finds it easier to acquire knowledge than someone older, often, perhaps, because he has less to unlearn.

But whatever you are, whatever age, whatever your ability, or whatever your sex (for despite the use of 'he' and 'him' for reasons of economy, this book is here for all) you can work your way through these instructions. If you understand what is asked of you in these pages – and, I believe, you should – then you can do it in your own time. How much time you are pre-pared to put into it is probably pro-portionate to how interested you are in the fascinating art of wrist-spin.

Finally, though this book covers the fundamentals, it does progress to a post-graduate stage. There is valuable information here, I believe, for the first-class and Test wrist-spinner as well as the beginner, or the experi-enced club bowler. So use it as is appropriate, understanding that you are not expected to absorb it all in one sitting, or even in one normal career.

CHAPTER 3

Eight Stages of Spin

In all cricket – indeed in life as a whole – there are many different ways to achieve success. Many do things differently, and it is a foolish teacher or coach who under-rates the importance of individual differences. As a general rule, it is dangerous to interfere with individuality, unless it has created an impossible technique. So I am very wary of changing grips, actions, or indeed anything, until they have been long and carefully observed. *But, if there is one factor in spin bowling which all spinners should accept if they wish to perform to their optimum, it is the concept that the ball should be spun hard.*

Not rolled, not gently turned, but flicked, ripped, fizzed. If young bowlers learn to spin hard from the start, then bowl enough spinning it hard, they can achieve accuracy. Giving the ball a flick is never an excuse for inaccuracy.

So, my very first suggestion is that we spin the ball hard, we 'give it a flick'. How do we do that?

Fig 9   Spin it hard. Give it a flick.

Figs 10–11   Hold the ball in your right hand. Roll your fingers and wrist over
the top of the ball and propel it, across your body, to your left hand. You have
executed a leg-break.

STAGE ONE

Let's start simply. Stand up straight with both hands out in front of you – comfortably, with bent elbows. Hold the ball in your right-hand if you are right-handed. Now roll your fingers and wrist over the top of the ball and propel it, across your body, to your left hand. When you have done that, you have executed a leg-break.

Now let's try to spin the ball harder. Let's try to make our fingers and wrist flick harder as we twist over the top of the ball. Try to use every finger as another lever to help the spin, and make the wrist work hard, too, as another lever. Spin the ball ten times, twenty times. Try to spin it harder each time. Flick it, with all the wrist and all the fingers.

Now get your forearm and elbow involved too. And the shoulder. Think of each of these joints as more levers to help in the flicking spin action. Feel them working! Not just fingers. Not just wrist. But fingers, wrist, forearm, elbow and shoulder. Feel them work. Keep on spinning. From right hand to left hand (or vice versa, if you are left-handed) over the top, from right to left.

Figs 12–13 Note the half-ball grip, finger and wrist positions. The thumb is important for some bowlers, quite irrelevant for others.

You may like to experiment with the way you hold the ball – *the grip*. I have seen so many leg-spinners grip the ball differently, yet still bowl it effectively, the most important factor is that the grip is comfortable and suits you.

Even so, it is always sensible to understand 'the orthodox' method. For 'orthodox' simply means the way that suits most people. Whether you eventually choose to use the orthodox method or not, you should understand it, and experiment with it. Look closely at the illustration below.

You will note that:

- A cup has been formed by the hand with the little finger and third finger bent up.
- Half the ball fits into the cup so made.

Try the orthodox and spin. Try your own way if it is different. The most important thing is that you find the grip which makes it easiest for you to spin the ball hard.

Practising Spin

1. Every chance you can get, spin a ball – tennis ball, cricket ball, table tennis ball, hockey ball. Any ball. Apples and oranges should be spun too. Spin them a hundred times before you eat them, and they'll always taste a little better! Spin the ball in front of television. Spin it in the garden. Spin before you go to bed. Try to spin harder and harder. Try to feel what I mean when I say 'give it a real flick!'
2. If you are spinning it to yourself,

Fig 14   Now spin it back towards your chest.

garden, or even in the street. Now instead of spinning directly from hand to hand, spin the ball *under-arm* into the wall to bounce back to you. Notice how it bounces off the wall to you. Notice how it bounces off the flat surface between the wall and you. Do they turn in different directions? If so, why?

4.   Do the same with a *round-arm* action. Lengthen the distance to six or eight yards. Try it *over-arm*. But all the time you are spinning that leg-break hard, trying to use all 'the levers'.

try two methods. One is, as we have already discussed, spinning it from right-hand to left-hand. The other is to hold it out in front of your body and spin it back towards your chest.

.   I'll come back to that later. For the two described are different types of leg-spin, both important, and later you will need to understand and master them both. But, for the time being, simply spin away – some from right-hand to left; others from right-hand held out in front, back towards your chest.

3.   Find a wall which has a nice flat surface beneath it. Somewhere around a tennis court, or in a gym, maybe at home in the

Fig 15   Valuable under-arm practice. Note the angle of spin on the ball.

Fig 16   Spin it hard. Make it turn. Try to beat your partner.

. If you have trouble with over-arm, go back to round-arm; trouble with round-arm, go back to under-arm: trouble with under-arm, go back to hand to hand.

5. You've found a partner – friend, brother, sister, Dad! Stand about five yards apart and spin backwards and forwards to one another. See how far you can make the ball turn. See if you can confuse your partner.

. Try it under-arm, round-arm, over-arm. Lengthen the distance. Just keep on spinning. And remember, even though you have a partner now to share the fun, still keep on with the same old spinning practices when you are by yourself – from hand to hand, or against that wall.

6. Your partner has a bat. Bowl your leg-spinners to him over a short distance, then gradually longer distances. If you can only use a soft ball where you are, it is just as useful. Spin the ball hard and try to turn it past the bat. *That's your primary aim, and whilst you are a spin bowler, even if you reach Test cricket, that is what your primary aim should always be – to spin the ball past the bat.*

7. You have a group of players now. Of course, you can simply play cricket – 'bowls-out-goes-in' – and you will keep bowling your leg-spinners. In your imagination, be Shane Warne, or Ian Salisbury, or Abdul Qadir. Imitate them. Watch yourself in your mind's eye.

Fig 17   Compete. Beat them with turn. Spin it hard.

8.   Or you can divide the group into two teams. Stand them opposite one another, with feet outstretched, feet touching. Now spin one ball backwards and forwards between the teams, whoever catches it spinning it back. Your aim is to beat your opponent with turn and get the ball to go between his legs. Do that and you score a point. First team to ten points wins.

Remember as you carry out these exercises that *short distances* are a better learning process than a full twenty-two yards, particularly as you begin anything new. You get the same spinning practice over six yards or ten yards as twenty-two yards, but you can also see the ball spinning more easily over the shorter distance as you spin it, you can see your partner's wrist and fingers working more clearly, and, to begin with, you will be more accurate. You will come to expect accuracy.

Learn from watching carefully. Always watch the ball being spun in the opponent's hand; always watch the spin of the ball in the air. Such disciplines will become habits which will serve you well in cricket over the years.

STAGE TWO

So far, we have been spinning whilst standing still, concentrating on what the fingers, wrist, forearm, elbow and shoulder should do in order to spin the ball hard. Now it is time to add a run-up – the approach moving into delivery. At the moment, I am discussing these aspects – approach and delivery – primarily from the point of view of spinning the ball. There are other factors to be considered about

Fig 18 Bowling practice. You don't need a batsman. They just get in the way.

both approach and delivery, but we'll come back to those later (see Chapter 4).

Don't run up too far, that will make things more difficult for you – perhaps encourage you to bowl faster than is comfortable, or offer more time to make mistakes. Often with a longer run-up, you find yourself thinking about it, whereas it must be so much second nature that you do not think of it at all. Most bowlers begin with longer run-ups and, as time goes by, they cut them down. Not because they are old and tired or unfit, not because they are lazy, but simply because they come to acknowledge that they simply do not need them. Your run-up needs to be long enough to bring you to the point of delivery at a reasonable momentum, so that you obtain full body drive in your delivery. So to start with, let's try about five paces or so.

At the moment, I'm not concerned about a pitch, let alone twenty-two yards. Simply run up into a bowling position and bowl. Think of bowling positions you have seen others use, and have perhaps imagined yourself using. Run up and bowl into a wall, to a partner, any distance will do. Just run up and bowl. Watch other bowlers run up. Watch them on television. Look at the illustrations below. Then do it yourself.

Don't try to think too much about how you are doing it. Just run up, bowl and keep on spinning the ball hard. And try to be *rhythmical*. I emphasize rhythm because all good sportsmen tend to be rhythmical in whatever they do. Talented swimmers, athletes, gymnasts, footballers – they do what they do rhythmically rather than jerkily. And the same goes with bowling. So concentrate on rhythm rather than too much on where your feet and arms should go.

Don't necessarily try to bowl over

Figs 19–20   Bishen Bedi. Admittedly he is a finger-spinner, but the rhythm and the controlled relaxation of his action is a wonderful model.

twenty-two yards at this stage either. It may be five or six yards to start, later ten to twelve. Just run up and bowl over that distance to Dad or brothers, or into a wall if you like. Begin your approach with rhythm, move into a bowling position, bring over your arm and spin the leg-break as you have been practising for so long now. Keep on spinning it hard and try to aim it where you want it to go, but do not sacrifice spin to get it on target.

Bowl like this as often as you can, whether against a batsman, to another player or onto a wall. Bowl and enjoy spinning the ball hard. If you are by yourself, you may even enjoy chalking

Fig 21   Rhythm. Everything about the great Abdul Qadir is rhythmical.

out targets to bowl at just for added interest.

STAGE THREE

Don't be concerned about the particular pace you are bowling. Continue to do as you have previously. Run up with rhythm, move into a bowling position, and bring over the arm spinning the ball hard, using all the levers we have mentioned – fingers, wrist, forearm, elbow and shoulder. Bowl a couple now where you close your eyes and feel all those levers 'getting into the act'. It's not just fingers or wrist alone, is it?

There are a few other things to check on now you have reached this stage. A few other factors to help you spin. For, as well as fingers, wrist, forearm, elbow and shoulder, you need both arms and your entire body to create the power to spin.

Try this, with your eyes closed perhaps, watching yourself in your imagination. Lead your front shoulder at your target (Dad, brother, batsman, wall) lifting up your front arm high to lean your weight back on your back foot just before you deliver the ball.

Now as you begin to bring the bowling arm into play, and you begin to move your weight forward, make your front arm and your whole body join in the work of spinning. Feel the 'old levers' creating spin, but also try to feel this additional power coming from the work of both arms and your entire body.

Remember you are not a slow bowler, you are a spin bowler. During the delivery, your entire body will

Fig 22 Terry Jenner became an outstanding leg-spinner for South Australia and Australia. Terry's powerful wrist gave him great over-spin and bounce.

work just as hard putting spin onto the ball, as the fast bowler does putting pace on the ball. But whereas his power is straight behind the middle of the ball, yours is on one side. So there is almost as much explosive effort put in by the spin bowler but for a different reason. Just as you do not wish to roll out the spin with fingers and wrist alone, nor do you wish to neglect the power imparted by both arms and the whole body. Using all of this at the moment of delivery should cause you to grunt or almost grunt with the explosive effort involved.

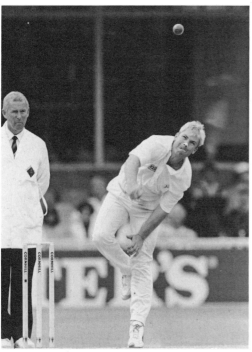

Fig 23   Look at the effort involved as Shane Warne releases the ball. Is he grunting? (Patrick Eagar)

Fig 24   Abdul Qadir pivots around the braced front leg and the bowling shoulder now faces the batsman. (Patrick Eagar)

As the bowling arm comes over, spinning hard with the entire body driving hard and forward, the front arm tucked into the ribs now, the back leg will pivot around the braced front leg, turning your body so that the bowling shoulder now faces the batsman. The effort of the delivery has turned you right around.

Automatically now, your momentum will carry you on forward for a few paces in what is called your follow through. The follow through is not something you 'tack on'. It must be the natural continuation of the body movement caused by the explosive effort of the body during delivery.

Now run up and do it several times. Shut your eyes, and watch your movements in your imagination. You are Shane Warne doing it. Or Tim May. Or Abdul Qadir. Feel everything working for you now in order to create spin. Fingers, wrist, forearm, elbow, shoulder, both arms, all your body at delivery – forcing that body pivot and follow through. You feel the power you are putting into it, all at the moment of letting the ball go, that final explosive effort that makes you grunt or nearly grunt, audibly or inaudibly. Keep working at it! Keep spinning it, flicking it, ripping it!

Once you are doing this, don't

worry about the pace of your bowling again. For once you are really giving the ball all you can, the pace it comes out naturally is the pace you should bowl. *That is your natural pace.*

If it is slower than some others, so be it. That's your style, and as a slower type you will have certain advantages and other disadvantages. If it is quicker than some, the same applies – advantages and disadvantages. Neither is the 'right way' to bowl. *There is no magically correct pace for a spin bowler.* They are simply different. And you will live, prosper or otherwise, by making the most of whatever pace is yours. But that is always assuming that you are using both arms and all of your body at delivery. Don't be one of those wrist-spinners who idles up to the crease, turns his arm over with no explosive power, simply lobbing it up in the air, with no body drive, no consequent pivot or follow through.

Such bowlers, and I have seen many (I call them 'hand-grenade lobbers'), often grow up quite successfully on concrete wickets. Their high lobber deliveries bounce up so high that only frantic tennis-like smashes can deal with them. But when they move to higher levels, turf wickets and more experienced batsmen, they have little to offer. They must learn to employ both arms, all their body, and explode through their delivery to discover what their natural pace is, if they are to have any future.

Now go away and bowl for a few years. Bowl anywhere – in the backyard, in the street, in the nets, in matches. Just bowl. And spin, spin, spin! And love it!

STAGE FOUR

It is now time to think a little more carefully about the type of bowling you have taken on. That is leg-spin, if you are right-handed; off-spin if you are left-handed. Wrist-spin! What you are doing is more difficult than most forms of bowling. But don't despair, for you have more than comparable advantages.

Fast and medium-pace bowlers bring their fingers and hands straight down behind the ball which should make accuracy easier to achieve. Spinners are spinning hard around one side or the other of the ball, which complicates accuracy. Even finger-spinners find it easier than you, for their method of imparting spin, dictated by the physical construction of the shoulder and arm, restricts the amount of leverage available compared to the wrist-spinner. *Only the wrist-spinner has the enormous leverage we have been describing and practising so far.*

It allows fascinating variations of spin, but, if you are making full use of it, it can make accuracy more difficult. More difficult, but never impossible. For it simply means you will need to put in more work and bowl more often to achieve accuracy. But, if you love it, the extra bowling should be no burden. That's what you enjoy most. Be assured, the accuracy will certainly come if you work at it and work *correctly* – something I shall discuss later. Wrist-spinners are not less accurate than any other bowlers – if they are prepared to work at it.

In return for this relatively minor problem, however, you receive more than ordinary advantages. As a wrist-spinner, you are blessed with *a range of spin variations* which are unique in the game of cricket. They give you the most fascinating and enjoyable type of bowling to pursue and a bag of skills and tactics that will interest, even enthral, you all your life. Let me explain!

For most people who watch and/or play cricket – often quite knowledgeable ones – spin is associated mainly with turn, that is, the ball's sideways movement off the pitch after contact. *Of course, turn is indeed one product of spin, but it is by no means the only one, and probably not the most important one either.*

Watching modern tennis on TV (or, when it happens occasionally, table tennis) can be the beginning of an interesting education for young wrist-spinners. Note the over-spinning drives, or over-spinning lobs. Note how the player hits over the top of the ball, thereby imparting maximum over-the-top spin. And what results from such over-the-top spin, or, as we shall call it from now on, over-spin?

Over-spin causes the ball to drop, particularly into a breeze. A clearly defined 'loop' results. And, as the ball descends more steeply, so it bounces higher. Thus over-spin creates drop and bounce. The drop also means that the over-spun ball will land further away from the batsman than a normal delivery – it has shortened its length.

Now watch the tennis player under-cut some of his drives. They appear to travel flatter than a flat-racket shot, far flatter than a loopy over-spun shot. It is more than a simple appearance. They do 'stay up' longer, flat-

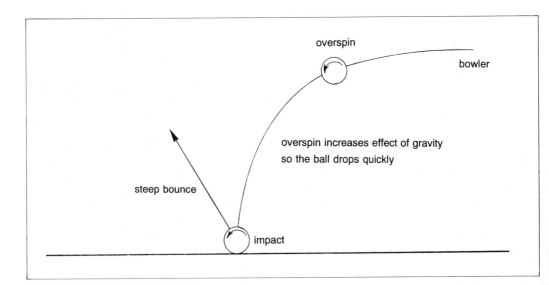

Fig 25   Over-spin causes the ball to drop quickly. The steeper descent causes steeper bounce. The ball lands further from the batsman than expected.

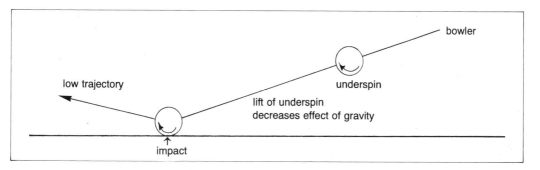

Fig 26   Under-spin or back-spin holds the ball up and flattens the trajectory. The ball lands closer to the batsman than expected. The lower bounce seems like 'skid'.

tening the trajectory of the ball. As a result, it makes contact with the court at a more acute angle, then bounces at a more acute angle. And, because it stays up longer it travels further in the air to land closer to the striker than it otherwise would. It has 'increased its length'.

This is all caused by under-spin, or back-spin – as it travels towards its target, it is spinning backwards. *Thus back-spin causes a flatter trajectory and consequent lower bounce or 'skid'. It 'goes on'.*

Not surprisingly, when over-spin follows back-spin, and vice versa, they further exaggerate the effects of one another.

Now what about side-spin in tennis? Watch the player slice the ball, particularly when serving. It is easier for the right-hand servers to slice on the right side of the ball, which in fact creates off-spin in a bowling sense. The serve drifts in the air from right to left. It drifts 'out'. For the left-hand server, it is easier to slice down the left side of the ball, creating 'leg-

spin'. The serve now drifts from left to right. It drifts 'in'. *The ball always drifts the opposite way to the eventual 'turn' after bouncing.*

Now watch the tennis player serving, when he combines side-spin and over-spin on the ball. The right-hand server cuts over and outside the ball (the right side of the ball) and creates a clearly defined out-drift, which also drops, then bounces high and spins back in the opposite direction to the drift. Vice versa for the left-hander.

The lighter tennis ball exaggerates the effect of such spin in the air, that is, drop, drift, or a flattened trajectory. But a baseball pitcher illustrates equally well what spin can do to a ball in the air, and his missile is almost as heavy and hard as a cricket ball. The pitcher's out-curve drop is off-spin combined with the over-spin. The knuckle ball uses over-spin, and there are other pitching variations created by spin. It is significant that the baseball pitcher cherishes all these variations, yet never bothers about what they do after hitting the ground. *His*

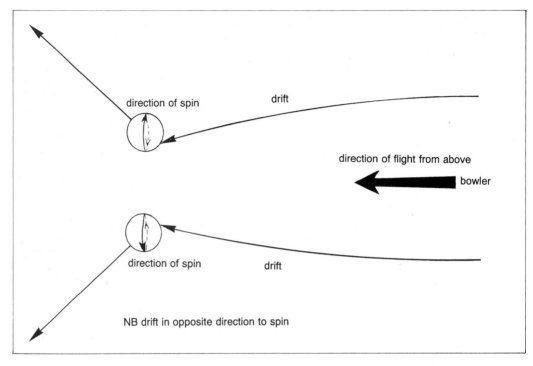

Fig 27   Drift is as important a product of spin as turn.

use of spin is entirely for its effect on the ball in the air.

The lesson is surely there for an intelligent bowler. Certainly spin creates turn, but it can do far, far more than that. It can offer the skilled experienced bowler drop, drift, bounce, flattened trajectory, skid, disguised varying lengths – as well as different angles of turn.

Now let's look at these ideas again from a practical bowling point of view.

Stand side-on in a bowling position with left shoulder facing your target (be it stumps, wall or Dad!). Now, using the leg-break spinning action we have been employing, spin the ball square across the target from right to left – the direction of spin would be towards point or backward point if the fieldsmen were there. As that ball hits the ground, it will turn in the direction of the spin; but not square, not at right angles, for its forward momentum will decrease the angle of turn. But, even so, this will be the largest angled leg-break that you will try to have available in your repertoire. That is your *big leg-break*.

Still in the same bowling position, prepare for another leg-break, but, this time, adjust your wrist to spin over the top of it a little more, so that the direction of spin is more towards gully or slips. When it hits the ground, the

Fig 28 The big leg-break is about to be released. For the reader's convenience the ball is being spun along the seam of a red and white ball.

Fig 29 Same spin, but the wrist has turned over a little more. Now it is a smaller leg-break – less side spin but more over-spin.

turn will follow the angle of spin to create a smaller leg-break. That is your *smaller leg-break*. It has some side-spin on it, but also quite a deal of over-spin. I won't pursue that yet, but a few readers who remember the tennis and baseball players may be getting a few ideas at this stage.

Prepare to bowl again, but this time turn your wrist so that you spin straight over the top. This creates a direction of spin straight towards the target. On hitting the ground, the ball goes straight on. That is your *over-the-top top-spinner. It has maximum over-the-top spin and no side-spin.*

So far, by simply turning the wrist to adjust the direction of spin, you have a big leg-break, a smaller leg-break and a top-spinner, all bowled with the same spinning action of fingers, wrist,

Fig 30 Same spin, but the wrist has turned over further. Now there is no side-spin; all over-spin.

forearm, elbow and shoulder. I call this *'going around the loop'* and you should practise it constantly. It is excellent spinning practice, and, at the same time, it is getting your mind to accept what the wrist must do to create three different and important variations. Practise it alone, standing or sitting, again with any type of ball, apple or orange. Make sure you continue to give it a good flick.

Now do it over a short distance towards a target or helper. But try to achieve the feeling of getting more *'round the side of the ball'*, more *'over the top'* and eventually *'right over the top'*.

As time goes by lengthen the distance until eventually you are 'going around the loop' over twenty-two yards. Keep to the back garden or nets as yet, but eventually, as you gain confidence, try it out in a centre wicket situation.

It makes sense that you should be able to understand what is involved, and, as such, it should be simply a matter of work and practice to master these three adjustments. And as you do so, think back to what we learnt about spin in tennis, table tennis and baseball. There is more to it than turn.

The ball you spin over the top – the over-spinner – will have no sideways turn but it will have maximum drop and bounce, and it will land 'shorter' than a normal delivery. The smaller leg-spinner will have some turn and drift from sideways spin, but some drop and bounce from the over-spin on it. The biggest leg-spinner, spinning 'square', will have maximum turn, as well as drift, but with no over-spin will not drop as quickly and will

therefore carry on to a 'fuller' length.

Surely that is fascinating already. But there is far more to come in later stages. Before we go on to the next stage, however, one last point about angles of spin so far.

Remember in Stage One, I spoke of the two types of spin practice as you begin. One where you spin from the hand in front of you back towards your chest, the other from the right hand over the top to the left hand. Well the first is maximum side-spin practice, the other is over-the-top-spin practice. Both are essential.

It is worth while pointing out here that most bowlers will begin doing one or the other of these more naturally. They will tend to bowl more out of the front of the hand, or more over the top. Neither is right, neither is wrong. One is simply side-spin, one over-spin. To be restricted to one or the other is a disadvantage, however, and the aim is, by practice, to be equally accomplished at either. Then you can bowl a big leg-break, smaller leg-break, and over-the-top-spinner at will.

STAGE FIVE

So you have been working at 'going around the loop' from biggest leg-spinner to smaller leg-spinner, to over-the-top-spinner. You have bowled them against the wall, to a partner, to batsmen, short distances, longer distances, in the nets and in the middle. You have conquered that, you are confident to bowl all three at will. Time to go on, then!

If you turned your wrist from square

Fig 31   Spin away. Keep on working. Think it out for yourself.

leg-spinner, around a few degrees to smaller leg-spinner, around a few more degrees to over-the-top-spinner, now turn the wrist a few more degrees. The ball will come out of your hand over the top of the little finger and third finger. It will have some over-the-top-spin on it, but, as well, it should have an angle of off-spin similar to the angle of leg-spin on your smaller leg-break.

You have just bowled a wrong'un, googly, or bosie. They are all the same ball – an off-break which looks something like a leg-break because of the fuller wrist turn involved. That it is called so many names indicates the sheer joy that so many bowlers have

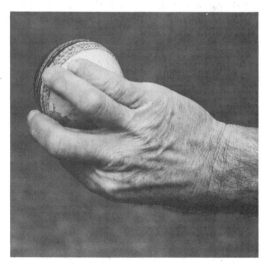

Fig 32   Same spin, but the wrist has turned further still for the wrong'un.

Fig 33   The big wrong'un – a larger angle of turn. The thumb has been left on the ball for this demonstration. Taking the thumb off the ball at delivery increases the flexibility of the wrist and enables you to give the wrong'un a bigger flick.

got from achieving it. It has been called many other names by batsmen who did not understand it or detect it.

Whilst we are at it, turn the wrist a few more degrees on if you have a supple enough wrist, and flick the ball over the little finger and third finger. This will create a large angle of off-spin with more side-spin on it and less over-spin. *So you have two googlies – a small one and a bigger one.*

Whilst practising these, start off from a few yards only – again to the wall or partner. Try to flick them rather than roll them. Some textbooks advise that you may need to drop your

left shoulder and open up the body to get the ball out over the top of the little finger in the wrong'un action. Possibly, to start with, but not necessarily. If you are really flicking with wrist, fingers, forearm, elbow and shoulder, they will cope with the necessary physical action with little change from the leg-break action. It is usually only 'the roller' who needs great adjustment, and, of course, with such adjustment, the wrong'un becomes very easy to detect.

As you experiment with the wrong'un, try taking your thumb off the ball. If your thumb keeps contact with the ball, it limits the flexibility of your wrist. For many, as soon as they forget their thumb in executing the wrong'un, a flick becomes far more possible and easier.

You may practise the wrong'un underarm to begin with. Stand six yards from the wall, bowl your leg-spin at the wall. You'll note it comes out of your hand on the inside, or left side of your arm. Now bowl the wrong'un and it will come out on the outside or right side of your arm. Spin away happily. Wrong'un, leg-break, wrong'un, leg-break. Now go round-arm. The leg-break will come out underneath your arm, the wrong'un above. Spin away merrily.

The advantage of both under-arm and round-arm is that you can watch your fingers and wrist in action. You can see if they are doing what you want them to, and the mind begins to accept what the joints must do to achieve the aim.

As soon as you go over-arm, this advantage ceases. It is difficult to see what is happening up there, and mind

Fig 34 The wrong'un bowled round-arm. See the position of the right hand and wrist.

and wrist can become confused. If you have trouble go back to round-arm; trouble there, go back to under-arm, and gradually work your way up.

If you understand what has been said – and the concept of 'going around the loop' should be logical – you can achieve your wrong'un with time, thought and practice. A little bit of individual help from someone who knows can speed it up, but you can do it alone.

One major warning! If you are working to achieve the wrong'un, don't forget your leg-breaks and top-spinners. *Don't bowl all wrong'uns for a week, or even a few days.*

For a grave danger that many have experienced is that they lose their leg-spinner. They become a bowler of all wrong'uns as their mind becomes confused. Believe me it does happen, it has happened frequently, and it is most frustrating. So first, try to avoid it by not bowling too many consecutive wrong'uns as you are learning. Leg-break, wrong'un, top-spinner, leg-break etc. Best of all, practise 'around the loop' from big leg-break to big wrong'un. Just keep on going.

But if, despite all this, you do lose your leg-break temporarily, you must set out to remedy this immediately. What you have to do is get the mind

Fig 35   The wrong'un under-arm. See it departing from 'outside' the hand and wrist.

Fig 36   The leg-break under-arm. See it departing from inside the hand and wrist. Watch the spin of the ball in the air.

to see what is going wrong, and thus overarm is *not* the way. Go back to underarm – leg-break, wrong'un – watching your hand and wrist at work. Go to round-arm, watching them at work. Keep at it, watching, identifying. Now go back over-the-top, watching in your mind's eye.

In my experience, this can overcome what for many has been a long-term and frustrating problem and for others even a terminal one. It is a little empty to be a bowler of wrong'uns who cannot bowl a leg-break and it can so easily be avoided.

There we are for the moment. You have 'going round the loop' to fill many an hour. Just sit there side-on in a bowling position spinning into a wall, or to a partner. Sit there spinning hand to hand. Increase your distances. Bring it into the nets, then the centre.

Force your mind to accept what your body and arm must do. Try to introduce the variations of turn so described into your normal bowling. For now you have available to you a big leg-break, a small leg-break, an over-the-top-spinner, a small wrong'un and a big wrong'un. With practice, you will be able to bowl them when wanted or needed. At will. Simply 'with a flick of the wrist', as it were.

If you remember the earlier description of the use of spin by the tennis player and the baseball pitcher, however, you should realize that the variation available to you is far, far more than the various angles of turn.

Your big leg-spinner and big wrong'un are 'square' spinners. They have maximum side-spin and minimum over-spin. They will give you drift in the direction opposite to the eventual turn, and they will turn furthest.

The small leg-break and small wrong'un will still turn, but less, for they have a smaller angle of side-spin. But they have over-spin. Hence they will drop more, bounce more, and land further from the batsman than expected.

The over-the-top-spinner has maximum top-spin, but no side-spin. It will go straight, but offer you maximum drop and bounce.

Think over all of that very carefully. Absorb it. You now have available a comprehensive armoury. You are able to turn the ball further or less as required. You are able to drift in either direction as required. You are able to create additional drop and bounce as required. How fantastic! Of course, this does not mean that you use all these variations each over. Some you may only use very occasionally – perhaps not at all in some innings. But if you work hard and master them they are there when you want them, when the situation, conditions or tactics call for them.

Let's take just one example. You are bowling to a batsman who reveals a weakness outside leg-stump. Let's imagine he is the type who is getting onto the front foot early, constantly looking to get at you to off drive and cover drive. Many such players commit their front foot well forward and across to the off before delivery. If a ball is suddenly bowled well up, wide of leg-stump, it is behind their initial commitment, particularly if it drifts in before it spins back. Usually when such a player then tries to play the sweep, his front leg remains on off-stump, or straight down the pitch, and the leg-stump is left exposed.

So the tactic is clear. Bowl up around off-stump and outside. Well up. Vary your drop, drift and turn. Encourage him to off drive and cover drive as he wishes to do. Wait, don't hurry. Be patient. Plug away.

Now having baited the hook, having encouraged him to off drive, having encouraged that early front foot commitment, deliver your biggest leg-break wide of leg-stump and full. You have encouraged a sweep shot, but the front foot commitment should have left the leg-stump exposed. He may well miss the ball. If so, landing in the rough wide of leg-stump and full, it will assuredly hit the stumps. If you can bowl the *bigger leg-break*, it will hit them even if two feet wide of leg-stump from the rough caused by the bowler's footmarks.

So you as a bowler recognized a batting weakness, gradually worked on it, baiting a hook, then struck. But in the long run, it could only succeed if you did have control of a bigger leg-break when required, and you could bowl it when and where you wanted it – that is accurately.

All this will be discussed again later, as we discuss accuracy, experience, and tactics, which combined with variations explain the development of the successful bowler. But for now, back to our spinning. 'Go round the loop', spin hard, 'give it a flick'. Work at it as hard and as often as you will. You cannot do too much, and you should be excited with what you are achieving. For already you have a bag of tricks, a variety of deliveries, which no other bowler can begin to challenge. Surely that's worth working for.

STAGE SIX

The Physics Explaining the Behaviour of a Spinning Ball

I am indebted to the excellent little book *The Physics of Ball Games* by C. B. Daish for offering a scientific explanation of the effects of spin on a cricket ball. The book is recommended reading for all ball-games players. What I have learned about the behaviour of a spinning ball in the air has come from a lifetime of observation, and it is encouraging that Daish's work supports my conclusions with a scientific basis.

In brief what he explains is that a spinning ball is acted upon by a transverse force known as the Magnus Force. The Magnus Force creates the out-drift for the off-break and the in-drift for the leg-break. It also causes the ball with top-spin on it to drop. On this subject, he adds, 'But the sharp

dipping of the (tennis) ball through the air near the end of its flight, which is produced by the Magnus Effect, means that it strikes the ground at a steeper angle than it otherwise would, *and that its downward velocity at impact is increased.*' Thus, on a hard surface, the ball will bounce more steeply and higher 'than it otherwise would'.

Finally he discusses 'bottom-spin' which is what I call 'back-spin' or 'under-spin'. His fascinating outline deals mainly with golf as he states:

The lift force (created by bottom-spin) is vital to the golf drive *and may well play an important part in the flight of other balls. It opposes, to some extent, the effects of gravity and so keeps the ball in the air longer than would otherwise be the case.* In the case of the golf drive, the lift generated by the Magnus Force in the early stages of flight is just about sufficient to balance the downward force on the ball due to gravity; that is to say, it is just about equal to the weight of the ball. This is why a well driven golf ball travels for some distance in practically a straight line.

Here he is dealing more with the flight of a golf-ball, but he does look at baseball and cricket. He does not mention the specific use of back-spin by the leg-spin bowler, but his explanations of the effect of bottom-spin on a golf ball are most relevant.

'Bottom-spin' (equals 'back-spin' equals 'under-spin') lifts the ball, and, though the additional mass of the cricket ball does not allow 'a straight

flight' as with a golf ball, or actual lift as with a table tennis ball, it does restrict the gravitational fall, thereby flattening trajectory, and by holding the ball longer in the air, increases length. The ball travels 'flat' and 'goes on'.

And because it makes contact with the ground at a more acute angle than normal because of the trajectory created, it comes off at an acute angle also. It 'skids' and 'keeps low' on a hard surface (although on a soft surface, the back-spin, in fact, is likely to dig in and 'hold up').

It only takes a little thought then to accept the complications created by side-spin, top-spin and back-spin 'round the side, over the top, and underneath'.

Inter-mixed, each type of spin further increases the apparent difference of the others. This enables the leg-spinner to build a confusing variety of deliveries which help to upset a batsman's judgement of length and line.

Some may scoff at the scientific discussion of the 'physics of the spinning ball'. Too theoretical, they may say. But we are all different, and for each person not impressed by such explanations, there will be another who is quite fascinated. Each to his own! From my point of view, as a coach, I firmly believe that it is easier to master something when you understand it fully, and part of understanding it should be why it all happens. If you understand 'why' and 'how' the rest should be up to you.

STAGE SEVEN

It is probable that experimentations in back-spin or under-spin amongst leg-spin bowlers began in Australia. There the wickets were hard and sun-baked, and leg-spinners with the ability to deceive batsmen with well disguised over-the-top-spinners or wrong'uns ran into unwelcome problems.

Let me explain. The wrist-spinner concentrating on off-stump line, turning his leg-spinner away has the obvious tactic of bowling a wrong'un or top-spinner to deceive the batsman. Now the ball comes straight on, or turns back from the off, rather than away to slips. Even if such deliveries are detected, they give the bowler a great chance of obtaining victims bowled or leg-before-wicket. When not detected, such chances are multiplied greatly. The better the batsman, the less chance of clean bowling him, as his defence becomes tighter, bat and pads closer. But this should not decrease the LBW opportunities unless . . .

And here is the unwelcome problem. The top-spinner and wrong'un have much over-the-top spin on them. Thus they drop quickly, and, on hard wickets, bounce more sharply and higher. Bowlers like Richie Benaud were frequently up into the batsman's ribs on good, hard wickets, and, of course, such bounce was a great bonus for the bowler. It is true to say that for the wrist-spinner, bounce is as important as turn.

But, in the case described, it also brought a disadvantage. The batsman was beaten by the wrong'un or top-spinner, but the bounce made any LBW or bowled decision most unlikely. Most unfair! Most frustrating! You had done the necessary work, perhaps deceived the batsman, certainly beaten the batsman, yet *he was saved by your skill*, your capacity to impart over-spin and make the ball bounce.

The next step was understandable. Wrist-spinners began to consider other alternatives. How could they achieve a straight ball or off-spin that could be disguised as a leg-spinner but kept low? Eventually someone came to understand the value of *back-spin* (bottom-spin, under-spin). If under-cut in tennis caused the ball to flatten trajectory, decrease the angle of bounce, and thereby skid on low, why not a bowled ball? Clarrie Grimmett, perhaps the greatest of all true wrist-spinners (I put O'Reilly in a different category) seems to have been the first to really exploit such a delivery in first-class cricket.

Grimmett developed the 'flipper'. Squeezed out of the front of the hand between thumb and fingers with the thumb underneath, this delivery had the flatter trajectory, the decreased angle of contact with the pitch which created 'skid' and 'keeping low', and, because the Magnus Effect kept it in the air longer, it 'went on', that is it landed closer to the batsman than first expected. It also sometimes squeezed back in from the off.

All of this, of course, because of back-spin. How was it achieved – still is achieved, if you watch Shane Warne carefully? Unlike all the other varieties mentioned so far, the 'flipper' is

Fig 37   Clarrie Grimmett. In the same era as Bradman, Grimmett's performances with the ball were as great as Bradman's with the bat. Perhaps the greatest leg-spinner ever, his arm action was low, and the leg positions shown here were quite unorthodox. But obviously it worked for him.

not created by wrist-spin action. As we have seen from big leg-break right round to big wrong'un, all are the same action, the same spin, except the wrist position is adjusted. To understand that was the point of 'going around the loop'.

No, the 'flipper' is quite different. Hold the ball out in front of you and spin it back towards your body. Normal wrist-spin, as we have been practising so long. Wrist and fingers over the top, all the levers working. Remember that is specific practice of side-spin, your biggest angle of leg-spin.

Keep on spinning it. See how it is spinning towards you. Now stop. Reverse the direction of spin. The thumb and index finger will begin the flick, away from you now, in the opposite direction to your leg-spin. So, it is an off-spin, but flicked. Again, use all the levers to flick it away from you. Keep flicking. Keep working. Keep watching. Note the spin now is going away from you.

When you have mastered this, put both hands out in front of you with elbows comfortably bent. That, of course, is the position you began with to roll your hand and fingers over the ball, propelling it from right-hand to left across your body, to create leg-spin.

Now perform that reversed spin described above, where the thumb and index finger begin the flick of spin opposite to leg-spin. Do that for a while in your right hand only, then propel it across your body from right hand to left hand. If you are following instructions, and doing it correctly, you will note that the ball is spinning backwards – it has underneath spin, back-spin, on it.

If you are having problems, go back to the beginning of this section on 'the flipper' and start again. But, if you have achieved the back-spin from right hand to left, across your body, you have succeeded in bowling a 'flipper'. Certainly, at this stage, it is only from hand to hand, but having got that far, as always, the rest is up to you.

Work from hand to hand, strengthening your wrist for the strain is quite

Fig 38 The flipper flicked out with the hand above the ball as Grimmett would have delivered it.

great. Gradually lengthen the distance, to a partner, to a wall. Persevere, be patient. If you can do it from hand to hand, you will master it over twenty-two yards, if you are prepared to work at it.

Grimmett apparently flicked his 'flipper' out with the seam more horizontal in flight. To do this required the hand on top of the ball, and thus a rather round-arm action. Whether the round-arm flipper dictated a rather round-arm action for everything else he bowled in order to help disguise it, or whether his round-arm action came first and the flipper followed that way, I have no idea. But the fact remains that Grimmett was very low-armed at delivery, which gave his 'flipper' its character.

Richie Benaud, on the other hand, was very high in his action at delivery. Richie did not introduce 'a flipper' into his repertoire until very late in his career, though he already had another back-spin in his bag of tricks – a beauty, which I shall describe shortly. But because of his high action Richie bowled his 'flipper' with the hand more inside than on top of the ball, thus creating an upright back-spinning seam. This caused the same back-spin effect as Grimmett's but, because the seam was vertical, the ball often swung in the air through seam effect – always in – creating an in-sliding skidder – a nasty delivery.

Every Australian leg-spin bowler I have seen, who was successful in first-class cricket, mastered some type of back-spinner, sometimes more than one. I would go so far as to say that it is unlikely that anyone without one will succeed at the top. I shall enlarge on that in Stage Eight.

Grimmett and Benaud had the 'flipper' and at least one other back-spinner. Bruce Dooland, a vastly admired bowler in England, had a superb 'flipper'. Cec Pepper, another great Australian leg-spinner who played most of his cricket in England, had his own speciality, a delivery he palmed out of the front of his hand which zipped off like a rocket. Outstanding Balmain and New South Wales leg-spinner, Reg Pearce, had one similar to Pepper's. Col McCool had another, which he was loathe to discuss, as was his son, Russell, who inherited it by word of mouth.

Outstanding wrist-spinners since Grimmett have all developed their back-spinner, some innovative ones amongst them, and almost all of these bowlers have persistently refused to discuss the mechanics of such deliver-

Fig 39   Richie Benaud moves into his perfect, side-on action. Look at his grip on the ball. It is probable that this photograph captured 'a flipper' about to be bowled. I wonder if they realized it.

ies. That's how important they were to them, and perhaps explains why so many non-wrist-spin cricketers were, and are, so totally ignorant of them.

Despite the innovators, however, most leg-spinners have relied upon a more orthodox back-spinner. This is the one I referred to with Richie Benaud, a delivery he bowled superbly and, at times, almost used as a stock ball. It is not difficult to understand the mechanics of this delivery, but, initially, it can be very difficult to achieve. Let me explain.

If you spin right over the top, you have an over-the-top-spinner, spinning straight ahead towards the batsman. A slight adjustment of the wrist creates a small angle of leg-break, retaining plenty of over-spin. Another wrist adjustment gives a square angle of leg-break with more side-spin than over-spin, and the wrist can be adjusted further to give total side-spin with no over-spin at all – a right angle of turn across the batsman. If you do not understand this, then you have not read the earlier stages of spin, or you have forgotten them. So go back to Stage Four and fully understand and master 'going around the loop'.

But now let's get on to the exciting part – one of the greatest thrills of wrist-spin. I want you to 'go around the loop' as above, from big wrong'un to big leg-spin. *Now think carefully! What if I continue that adjustment of the wrist just a degree or two further past the square leg-spin, still using the leg-break spin. The ball must have a certain amount of back-spin on it coupled with side-spin.*

This is the leg-spinner's dream ball. For it achieves the back-spin effect whilst still using the orthodox leg-spin action, and does so when angled a fraction away from the biggest leg-spinner you have.

On a firm wicket, such as most Australian wickets, the small amount of back-spin amidst the side-spin, is enough to create all the back-spin effects – flatter trajectory, 'going on', 'skidding'. Its only disadvantage is on a softer wicket. For then, the ball digs in, slows up, and spins square, whereas 'the flipper' still behaves itself.

Mind you the behaviour of the back-spinner on a soft wicket, described above, can be another useful variation, but, unless you have 'the flipper' also, you lack the skidding straight one in such conditions. Thus it is preferable to master both, if possible. Bruce Dooland and Cec Pepper assured me of the importance of a 'flipper' in English conditions because of prevalent softer wickets.

A quick re-vamp of the orthodox back-spinner. 'Go around the loop' to your biggest angle of leg-spin, simply spinning from one hand to the other. Now try to adjust a little further than square leg-break, and see if the ball has a small angle of back-spin amidst the side-spin leg-spin. You do not require total back-spin.

Once again bowl this from hand to hand, then into a wall, or to a partner over a short distance, then ever increasing distances. Your major problem as you increase the distance will be a mental one. *Your mind has to accept that you are spinning slightly backwards as your bowling arm goes forward.* That can be quite a problem. But keep at it over short distances and gradually the penny will drop, even if you need to half throw it in the early stages.

A warning! Again! Some instructions describing the orthodox back-spinning leg-break suggest that you push it out of the front of the hand, with the ball coming out between second and third fingers. Though that is an accurate description of what eventually happens, it can be confusing advice. For following that advice bowlers simply palm the ball out of the front of their hands, so obviously different from their leg-spinner, and without any real flick.

But, if, on the other hand you continue 'around the loop' flicking the same leg-spin action using all the levers, and eventually working past the square leg-spin, you continue to spin as usual. The delivery is more difficult to detect, it has real spin on it, and the faster rotating back-spin emphasizes the Magnus Effect. So there you are!

I do not believe these variations of spin are difficult to understand. For those who understand, they are far easier to detect from the hand. And detection from the hand is far preferable for batsmen than from spin in the air, or off the pitch.

Any intelligent all-round cricketer should 'pick' from the hand whatever wrist-spinners can bowl. Far too many batsmen do not 'pick' wrist-spinners. Even first-class batsmen. Even Test batsmen. Their first step in overcoming such a serious weakness is to understand how it works. Once you understand 'how' and 'why', it is amazing how suddenly and quickly you see it all happen in the hand at the moment of delivery. Suddenly you say, 'How did I ever fail to pick that?' I have seen several batsmen who have clearly revealed lack of knowledge of a leg-spinner's variety. Some of these were wonderful players.

I have also read books and articles or listened to television and radio commentators, which have emphasized lack of understanding which was surprising. One was a book written about Benaud's 'flipper' by experienced Test cricketers who should have known better. They discussed his 'flipper' long before he had one, and made it so clear that they could not differentiate between 'flipper' and orthodox back-spinner. The same happened with Shane Warne in 1993 in England. Batsmen were confused by his 'flipper', but so were commentators. For, on several occasions, Warne bowled an orthodox back-spinner which was nominated by eminent commentators as a 'flipper'.

Such confusion is fatal for a batsman, if not a commentator. There is no point 'picking' some of a bowler's deliveries; it must be all or nothing. A little knowledge can be a very dangerous thing, in this regard. If you cannot identify everything a bowler bowls, then you must assume you cannot 'pick' any. Then you simply watch hard, watching spin in the air, using your feet to kill spin, attacking anything short or full, and playing the rest off the pitch.

But it is far preferable to be able to pick a bowler from the hand. It gives you confidence and a great advantage in time. If you understand how and why things happen, watch the ball carefully in the hand, watch the spin in the air carefully, watch any new bowler or type of delivery you come across carefully – and think, think, think, you will come across very few deliveries that you cannot identify immediately. And you get better as time goes by.

Any self-respecting wrist-spinner should pride himself on recognizing anything another wrist-spinner bowls. For batsmen and wicket-keepers there is even more than pride involved. There is a serious matter of survival.

STAGE EIGHT

Over the years, I have often watched wrist-spinners who appeared to be bowling beautifully, yet were not taking wickets. They were on line and length, accurate, turning the ball nicely, and even offered the occasional wrong'un. But they did not even appear to be worrying the batsmen.

They were 'too predictable'. Sometimes these were bowlers spinning over-the-top and looping nicely; others were predominantly out of the front of the hand with side-spin. As I say they appeared to be bowling well, yet batsmen were able to get into position quickly either forward or back without hesitation in their footwork, and consequently with few major concerns.

Then an apparently less immaculate wrist-spinner bowled and began to inter-mix over-spin, side-spin and back-spin. Immediately the certainty of the batsman's footwork decreased. His feet stuttered forward, then hurriedly back; or back, then late and nervously forward. He was beginning to have greater problems in judging the length of the ball.

Judgement of length is the initial task of batting. As the batsman waits for the bowler and the ball, he stares at the ball. At the very moment of delivery, he is staring at the ball, so that his eyes and mind are able to make an instantaneous judgement of line and length.

Once that judgement is made, the body carries out the tasks of batting technique without thought; they are all drilled automatic reactions. But they are all dependent on that initial decision, that initial judgement of length. The speed of that decision is the greatest difference between the various levels of batsmanship. It explains why great players have so much time, why good players have more than average, and so on.

So a bowler's major task is to confuse, slow down, or destroy a batsman's judgement of line and length. A pace bowler may do that with sheer pace, or pace plus swing. A slow bowler does it with spin – **not 'turn' but 'spin'**!

And by now you should fully understand what I mean by that. Over-spin will create a looping flight, and the ball contacts the ground further from the batsman than he originally expected. But he will counter that given time. If, however, back-spin and side-spin are inter-mixed with over-spin, further complications occur, which reinforce and further emphasize one another, and can be fatal to a batsman's judgement of length. For some 'come on', some 'drop', and some 'drift'. That is what is meant by 'flight', a terribly misunderstood word which many think is simply throwing the ball up into the air. Any fool can throw it up, it is what happens to it up there that matters, and that comes from the mastery of over-spin, side-spin and back-spin.

Confuse the batsman's judgement of length and line, and the final effects of spin, off the pitch, finish him off. These effects are bounce, skid or

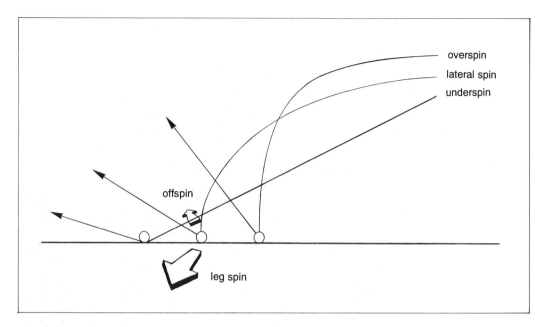

Fig 40 'Round the side', 'over the top', 'underneath'. The inter-mixture of spin which can confuse a batsman's judgement of length.

turn. Note 'turn' is only one of these, and note that primarily it is 'finishing off' what the other effects of spin have caused in the air before the ball bounces. Think back to our tennis player and baseball pitcher.

Of course, 'turn' is important, but it is not the be all and end all of spin bowling. Often those who do not understand this encourage bowlers to bowl faster to obtain 'faster turn'. Though there will be occasions when you bowl faster than normal for a particular reason, to do so regularly negates all your advantages. For to obtain just fractionally faster turn, you become flatter and lose drop, drift and bounce – all those ingredients likely to confuse judgement of length.

To sum up! Spin is what spin bowling is about, but spin is far more than turn. Sideways spin, should be varied and inter-mixed with over-spin, and back-spin. All of these, interwoven, create the spinning web into which experienced spinners are trying to lure and destroy batsmen.

So spin on, my friends! Spin on! Understand what has been said in these eight stages of spin, and work hard at putting it into practice. If there are final matters to fix in your mind about spin, they could well be: 'Spin hard! Give it a flick! Over the top! Round the side! Underneath! Around the loop!'

So, spin – spin and be merry, for tomorrow we may be seamers! A morbid thought!

Fig 41   So spin, spin and be merry!

CHAPTER 4

How to Be a Successful Bowler

You should have realized by now that I firmly believe spin is what makes spin-bowling different and it is what can make it so fascinating. But spin alone cannot make you a successful bowler. You need accuracy, variation, experience, knowledge, planning and tactics. These can take you from the category of a fine spinner of the ball to that of a successful spin bowler.

So let us progress. What is needed to become a successful bowler? First look at the following summary:

1. Attitude.
2. Accuracy.
    (a) Concentration.
    (b) Self-confidence.
    (c) Practice.
    (d) Action.
3. Power.
4. Variations.
5. Experience, knowledge, tactics.

And now let's expand that summary.

1. ATTITUDE

The key to it all! You have little chance of success without a sincere enthusiasm, even love, for cricket in general and spin bowling in particular. With such an attitude, the work involved –

and there will be a great deal of that – is no burden, it is a joy.

When I explain to people that from the age of six to sixteen, I played cricket most days, in holidays all day, many respond with 'you must have been dedicated'. It is clear that they do not begin to understand. For I was not at all dedicated, in my mind. I was, in fact, being selfish. I was doing what I enjoyed most.

I am afraid that if you wish to succeed as a spin bowler that will be an essential prerequisite – that you not only enjoy doing it, but probably enjoy it more than anything else. You cannot fake that, and you certainly cannot fool yourself. *Enjoyment is the basis of success*. Enjoy what you do, and you will relax. Relax and you will perform. Perform and you will obtain satisfaction. Obtain satisfaction and you will enjoy. And so on! Break that chain somewhere and you are in trouble. But try to start without the initial base of 'enjoyment' and there is simply nowhere to go.

This is true of amateur or professional. Professional sportsmen who have lost the enjoyment are easily distinguishable. The lack of enthusiasm from such players is an absolute certainty to turn off spectators, and one of the major responsibilities of a professional cricketer is to entertain those spectators. But it is not only harmful to the spectators and the game, it is harmful to the player himself. For, without enjoyment and enthusiasm, relaxation and performance become almost impossible goals.

Enjoyment, enthusiasm! They are closely linked to so many other vital ingredients – 'guts', determination, application, fitness, strength. They also help us to handle so many mental factors which can often destroy the most talented of players. Factors such as stress management, relaxation, concentration, confidence, perspective – all of which shall be dealt with in Chapter 5, 'Mind and Body'.

At this stage, let it be enough to say that when you no longer enjoy what you are doing in sport, you should get out – for the sake of the game, the sake of the spectators, the sake of your team-mates, and the sake of yourself. You must enjoy bowling to be successful. Enjoy spinning. Love spin bowling!

It is also vital that you try to excel, that is try to do the very best you can with the ability you have been given. Trying to do your very best at all times is what makes any sport so enjoyable – or life, for that matter! *For the essence of competition is competing against yourself, trying to obtain the optimum performance out of yourself.* When you achieve this, it gives you great satisfaction. It also means you have won a victory – a victory in achieving your personal goals, which is more important in the long run than any mere figures, points or partnerships.

So enjoy it, and never be afraid to show you enjoy it. Let others enjoy your enthusiasm. Set out to do your very best, and make the most of what you have. With such an attitude achieved, you are successful. Add some more skills and you will be increasingly so.

2. ACCURACY

A bowler with accuracy but no variation is limited; a bowler with accuracy but no real spin is not a spin bowler; but a bowler with spin and variation but no accuracy is nothing.

Accuracy is essential. With it and sensible variation amidst a plan, a bowler can accumulate pressure on a batsman. *If the bowler can apply more pressure on the batsman than the batsman can on the bowler over a period of time, then the bowler will win the contest and vice versa.*

There is no point in having all the spin and variations at your disposal, and the ability to recognize a batting weakness, unless you can put the ball where you want it when you want it. And that means accuracy. Nor is there an excuse for inaccuracy simply because you are a wrist-spinner. That is a let-off and a false one.

Bad wrist-spinners are inaccurate, but so are bad medium-pacers and quicks. Good wrist-spinners have always been accurate – *pin-point accurate*. From Grimmett and O'Reilly to Benaud, Higgs, to Warne – good wrist-spinners have been renowned for their accuracy. So get it out of your head that wrist-spinners 'are allowed' to be inaccurate. That is a very dangerous and false assumption which is often at the root of inaccuracy. If you believe you are likely to be inaccurate because you are a wrist-spinner, then you probably will be. But if you know that hard work and concentration will achieve accuracy, must be achieved if you are to be successful, then you can and will achieve it.

So what can we do to help achieve and improve our accuracy? It is often assumed that the bowler's action is likely to be the major factor in his achievement or non-achievement of accuracy. I question that strongly and suggest that *incorrect concentration techniques and incorrect and inadequate practice* are by far the major causes of inaccuracy. When bowlers learn what concentration is and carry out these lessons fully, then practise as often, as much and as correctly as they should, they rapidly grow in self-confidence. They begin to 'know' where the ball will go rather than 'expect' or 'hope'.

It is very seldom that the bowler's action alone causes inaccuracy. Seldom are the approach, delivery and follow through so incorrect that they limit accuracy, provided the bowler has correct concentration, practice and confidence.

It may sound pedantic to be so concerned with the order of importance in the causes of something so vital. I don't think so. For one of the major reasons for the loss or semi-loss of concentration which leads to inaccuracy is the bowler's concern with his action as he bowls. It is essential that bowlers understand that it is most unlikely that their action is causing the problems. Then they can forget about it, as they always should, and put their minds to the more important things which are likely to solve any problems they may have.

What I am saying is that far too much time and thought can be spent on the theory of a bowler's action, and this is often counter-productive. I shall expand on that possibly controversial comment later. But to go on!

(a)   Concentration technique

This is the major factor in improving accuracy and it is very much 'of the mind'.

(b)   Self-confidence

This is also a mental matter. Both concentration and self-confidence are therefore dealt with in Chapter 5, 'Mind and Body'.

(c)   Practice

Practice is the next most important factor. As a wrist-spinner you cannot bowl too much. You are not like a fast bowler, where too many hours of bowling can cause physical damage. The only damage you are likely to do by 'over-bowling' is to lose some skin off your spinning fingers, and though painful at times, it has seldom been terminal. Besides, as the old spin-bowlers' adage goes, 'Those that never bleeds, has never spun!' (best said with a West Country accent!). So be reassured that the longer and more often you can bowl your wrist-spinners, the more likely you are to be successful and certainly the more likely you are to be accurate. With one important proviso! You must expect to practise '*correctly*'.

You see, 'practice does not make perfect'. Constant repetition alone is not enough. It is '*perfect practice* that helps to make perfect'. The emphasis must be that you practise correctly. And that needs some explanation.

Perfect practice certainly does not mean that you must have perfect wickets to practise on. If you are lucky enough to have good centre wickets or immaculate nets to practise on good luck to you, and don't waste them. But the good conditions are not the most important factor at all. More important is that your approach to practice is serious, positive and purposeful. Spinning practice from hand to hand or against a wall is valuable practice. Bowling in the back-yard, the street or school playground is valuable practice, whether there is a batsman or not. But in all of these circumstances, regardless of the quality of conditions, *you must do it seriously and properly.*

Once you are warmed up, always measure out your run-up. Always run up with your normal approach, emphasizing rhythm; insist on your normal delivery, explosive power to spin the ball, and follow through. Above all, concentrate totally, as you would in the most serious match. What 'total concentration' means is not as straightforward as you may believe, many really have little idea what 'concentration' is, but this I shall discuss fully in Chapter 5. For the time being, however, I put it to you that unless you are concentrating totally during practice sessions, you are wasting your time.

Of course, part of the reason for practice is fun and enjoyment, but if it is to be worth while it must not be a joke or shambles. Once a bowler sets himself to bowl, then begins bowling, he cannot be talking, or laughing and joking – all his concentration must be on the task in hand, ball by ball – clearing his mind, watching his target, and 'thinking within the circle' (*see* Chapter 5).

No fellow bowler should talk to you once you set yourself, and you should not talk to your colleagues once they set themselves. General mucking around simply cannot take place during a real practice situation. All that happens then is that you become better at doing things poorly – which is another way of saying 'getting worse'.

None of us can get enough practice as wrist-spinners, let alone too much. So none of us can afford to waste practice situations by fooling with them. Do them properly, treat every ball like a Test match. Then every ball you bowl is likely to be improving you as a bowler. Of course you want to enjoy your practice, but enjoyment does not mean mucking around and wasting your time and everyone else's. Few of us get joy out of 'hit and giggle' situations.

As a wrist-spinner you should try to bowl as long as possible at practice. One hour of bowling is only a warm-up; try to keep the ball if you can; try to bowl right through the session. If you are forced to make way for another bowler, you can still bowl meaningfully to another player out of the nets – preferably the wicket-keeper, or simply into a wall or side-net. Your aim must be to chalk up *'bowling hours'.*

If you are not lucky enough to have practice conditions which allow you to bowl long spells (up to two and three hours), it is up to you to be innovative and create bowling situations such as I have already described. Don't give in, grumble about not getting enough bowling, and bow to an unpopular inevitable. *You* do something; improvise, don't make excuses.

If you are blessed with favourable conditions, use them well and don't waste them. If you are able to bowl uninterrupted for hour after hour, your problem is to maintain interest, discipline and concentration. Too many bowlers bowl for half an hour then come off 'tired' or stay on only half-concentrating. They are not 'tired'; more often they are bored, because they are practising unintelligently and without purpose. They warm up, then begin to try and bowl the batsman out and that's it. That is all they think of doing and their interest soon wanes.

Don't let that happen to you. Break your practice up; keep it interesting with specific aims. For instance, after you have warmed up, and begun to practise seriously (measured approach, rhythm, concentration etc.) simply bowl at the batsman for fifteen minutes. Then mentally set a field, planned for attacking middle and off-stump, and bowl again for fifteen minutes keeping your figures. Next, switch line to leg-stump, adapt the field placements and keep figures.

Now bowl an over or two where you experiment with new deliveries. It may be a wrong'un, over-spinner,

flipper, or back-spinner. At this stage, too, they may not be wonderfully accurate, but you have to practise them somewhere and that is one reason for nets. *Net practices are not for batsmen only, and the sole purpose of bowlers in nets is not to give batsmen good practice.* Never be embarrassed to set aside a few overs for experimentation. But not too long. After a fifteen-minute session, go back to simply bowling; try to get batsmen out. Then do some 'spot bowling'. This means changing line and length for each successive ball for a few overs – a top-spinner short outside off-stump; a bigger leg-break full and wide of leg-stump; a normal leg-break on length and line of off-stump, and so on.

I shall not pursue this any further. The purpose is clear, I hope, and the possible variations many. I have tried to break up my bowling into meaningful sections (the 'fifteen minutes', of course, is not obligatory), have concentrated on different skills and kept things interesting for me. Thus after two or three hours I am still bowling quite fresh because both mind and body are fully involved.

In this way I receive *'total practice'.* I get the necessary work for strength and fitness – for the best way to get fit for bowling is to bowl enough. I am working on correct technique; I am practising my concentration – the most important practice; and I am practising my accuracy and variations. At the same time, all the time, I am watching batsmen in my net and the other nets, learning and analysing, thinking how I would bowl to each, trying to recognize strengths

Figs 42–43 Graham McKenzie – a beautiful, rhythmic, copy-book action. It worked for him.

and weaknesses, planning tactics to best deal with these. Thus I am constantly expanding my knowledge and experience.

Each practice is a work-out for mind and body. If either is not involved fully, you are practising poorly. You should expect to practise hard, to work hard, and come away tired but satisfied. You have done something worthwhile, you have enjoyed it and you have made progress somewhere. Every practice!

So we cannot practise too much as long as it is perfect practice. It does not always have to be on centre wickets or in perfect net situations; be prepared to improvise and innovate. But always do it properly wherever you are. Don't waste time or opportunity; don't muck around. Enjoy it, but enjoy trying to make progress most of all. For most of us, correct concentration and practice will give the desired accuracy.

(d) Action

The bowling action may be divided into three components: the approach, delivery and follow through, but each must flow rhythmically into the other.

Figs 44–46   Max Walker – an ugly, jerky, unorthodox action. It worked for him.
Why change?

It is important to see the action as a 'means' to an end. In the context we are now discussing, the 'end' is the achievement of accuracy. Thus an elegant, attractive or orthodox action is unimportant in itself; our major concern is achieving accuracy.

If that can be done successfully with a natural action that is not orthodox, so be it. It is preferable that each individual gets the most out of his own individual method of doing something, rather than trying to create an assembly line of clones identical in their orthodox perfection. What might Bob Willis or Max Walker have lost if someone had tried to make them orthodox textbook bowlers? They benefited from the unorthodoxy that made them different.

So if you are achieving accuracy with your own methods, even if they are ugly or against textbook rules, don't change. You are achieving your end, so the means are unimportant. On the other hand, if your action is orthodox or unorthodox and you are not achieving accuracy, there may be a need for change. But, first, before you consider such change, examine parts (a), (b) and (c) of accuracy above. They may be what are at fault rather than your action.

Once it becomes quite clear that your action is so incorrect that it is causing the troubles, you will prob-

Fig 46.

ably need to alter it, to correct it towards the orthodox. For the 'orthodox' is simply the way that is best for most, and every cricketer should understand it, even if not needing to fully utilize it.

As I have said before, I am wary of over-emphasizing the mechanics of the action for nothing is more destructive than bowlers 'watching themselves' whilst bowling. It is the certain way to lose concentration and self-confidence. So I shall limit my discussion to the following:

APPROACH

Avoid an over-long approach. It creates too much opportunity and time to make mistakes, and, particu-larly for the wrist-spinner, can encourage him to try and bowl faster than is natural. There is a tendency, when you are younger, to run too far. It is significant that most bowlers cut their run down as the years go by, simply because they come to realize that they do not need them. The shorter run-up often encourages a bowler to relax and not push and force himself too hard.

Avoid too short an approach. If the run-up is too short, the delivery can lack body drive. No momentum has been built up, and the delivery lacks 'oomph'.

Be comfortable and natural. Don't 'watch' yourself trying to ape the orthodox. Relax and be yourself.

Be rhythmical. Rhythm is the key throughout approach and delivery. All successful sportsmen in any field tend to be rhythmical rather than jerky. It is part of seeming to have so much time and doing things easily.

My advice is that during your approach the only factor in it that you should be aware of at all is your rhythm. Forget what your arms, legs, shoulders and body should be doing. If your rhythm is right, they will look after themselves. For this reason it is a worthwhile exercise at practice – *but only when you are bowling well* – to 'listen' to your approach, visualize your run-up, and 'hear', 'feel' and 'see' the rhythm of your bowling. Mine was '1, 2–3, 4–5'. Others are quite different. What is yours?

Awareness of your own personal rhythm when you are bowling well becomes valuable when you are not. Rather than worrying about where your arms or feet are – something that

Fig 47   Abdul Qadir. Everything is so
rhythmical, even when frozen. Look at him
winding himself up.

often happens when things are not
going well – concentrate only on your
rhythm. Get your rhythm back to what
it should be, and, more often than not,
feet go back into place, arms go back
into place, the body does its job and
it all comes back together. Then you
can forget about your approach, as is
always the case when you are bowling
well.

Run through straight into delivery.
That does not mean *not* to run in to

your mark at an angle. Angling in
does make it easier to get side-on if
you need help to do so, though it does
delay the moment when you can look
along the line you wish to attack. By
'running through straight' here, I
mean continuing all your forces along
the one line, chasing the ball, not falling away in the final strides. Nothing
is more likely to upset your balance,
and thereby interfere with consistent
accuracy, than such final falling away.

The purpose of your approach is to
bring you to the delivery position balanced and controlled with adequate
momentum to put the required
'oomph' into your delivery. Don't
become too analytical or complicated. It is working for you if you feel
relaxed and comfortable, just let it
happen, and wipe the approach right
out of your head as you bowl.

THE DELIVERY

As a wrist-spinner, your major concern is that you are bowling with both
arms, your entire body and action,
that these create 'oomph' to explode
through the crease.

It is true that most successful wrist-
spinners have had textbook orthodox
actions – in the rhythm of approach;
the side-on action with high lifted
front arm and back feet parallel to the
crease; the transfer of weight from
back to forward; a rotation of
shoulders towards the batsman; a
delayed tuck-in of elbow to ribs to
maintain side-on delivery; an
explosion of effort through the crease;
a full two-armed and whole body
delivery; a pivot around a braced
front leg; and a strong follow through.

Fig 48 Ian Salisbury. The action is orthodox, but there is a stiffness and military precision about it. It does not have the natural, fluid grace of a Warne or Qadir.

Most have had that orthodoxy, perhaps more so in wrist-spin than any other form of bowling. For, more than any other form of bowling, the wrist-spinner with the fundamental difficulties involved in what he is trying to do, benefits from the safety-valves available in the orthodox action.

The chest-on bowlers, the one-armed bowlers, the past-the-vertical bowlers – they do not have such safety valves. There is nothing to fall back on if things go a little wrong, and then the 'wheels fall off' altogether. And,

alas, in the realm of wrist-spin, things have been known 'to go a little wrong' on occasions.

By no means am I suggesting that we immediately change every wrist-spinner to total orthodoxy of action. If he can handle his particular unorthodoxy, let him go. But beware!

Despite my wariness of becoming too involved in the technical and mechanical, there are several matters associated with delivery and wrist-spin which should be outlined. I do so with two warnings.

To the bowler. Think about the technical guidelines below, talk about them, visualize them, and sometimes work with them in practical situations. But never let them enter your head when you are bowling in a match.

To the coach. When it comes to his action, the bowler cannot see himself, and your role becomes particularly important and responsible. Be as knowledgeable as you can be, but do not push theory or orthodoxy on your charges unnecessarily.

Encourage the natural; avoid change for the sake of change, appearance or orthodoxy. Come to understand and appreciate the advantages and disadvantages of 'unorthodoxy' in various phases of the game as much as you understand and appreciate 'orthodoxy'.

Never try to change anything, unless, after long observation, you *know* it is essential to do so. Remember that 'it is always easier to muck someone up than it is to improve them by change'.

And when it comes to a bowler's

action, do not manufacture or half-imagine imperfections in his action and so create doubts. Leave his action alone unless there is something so incorrect that it is certain to cause inaccuracy. Always let the bowler know at once when you feel his action is all clear.

With these provisos, I outline the following thoughts on the delivery which could prove of value to you.

Many bowlers move into a perfect side-on position, then fractionally before delivery throw the front arm away too quickly. This opens the chest up too early, wasting the advantages of the initial side-on position, and causes the bowler to fall away off balance. He begins to sling and spray down both sides of the wicket.

This is very common and can be difficult to detect at first because his action looks perfect as he sets himself. But, if from that perfectly orthodox position, he is inaccurate, check for the symptoms outlined above. If they are there, they become very obvious once you identify them. Now attempt the following remedy.

The shoulders during the delivery should rotate over one another in a line towards the batsman, not around one another towards gully or point. Thus the body chases the ball rather than falling away.

To help this, the front arm coming down from the 'reach for the sky' position should tuck into the ribs before it is thrown away. Both of these aids will keep the bowler in his side-on position that little longer.

The side-on position is the orthodox

Fig 49 Jim Higgs moves into the orthodox delivery position for a leg-spinner.

position because it has built-in safety valves. The bowling arm from this position is like a wheel rotating towards the batsman. Whenever it is let go, the ball will at least go straight, on the correct line, and only letting it go at the correct moment in order to achieve the desired length remains a problem.

But the arm rotation of the slinger I have described above has no safety valves. During rotation, the ball released early sprays down the leg-side; late it goes down the off. All this is magnified by his lack of balance and falling away.

Fig 50   Mike Procter illustrates the 'past-the-vertical position'. But he was able to control it. Many cannot. (Patrick Eagar)

Bowlers who 'go past the vertical'. These are most common amongst leg-spinners and in-swing bowlers and are often combined with the hop which is sometimes, and usually incorrectly, referred to a 'bowling off the wrong foot'. I have seen only one bowler who did bowl with 'the wrong foot' forward at the moment of delivery, and that was Victorian left-hander Bob Bitmead. The majority of so-called wrong-footers, are hopping and jerking, but, carefully observed, have the normal foot forward at delivery.

When such bowlers 'go past the vertical', they usually overstretch backwards and become off balance, and one remedy is to stand them up straight, keeping their head and body upright, by getting the bowling arm back to a vertical position or even more round-arm than that.

Don't misunderstand me. Don't inte-fere if they are coping with this delivery, that is, if they are bowling accurately. 'Froggy' Thompson of Victoria, Mike Procter of South Africa, and Max Walker of Victoria and Australia were all 'past the vertical' bowlers, but controlled it, and gained great advantages from their unorthodoxy. But many bowlers who deliver this way lose balance and control. Usually they stray short and down the leg-side. A disaster!

To help them find a remedy requires some interesting information. Such bowlers have no idea where their arm is, that is they are not aware that they have gone past the vertical. If you talk to them and ask them where they believe their bowling arm is, almost without exception, they believe it is straight over the top. This is essential knowledge for any coach to understand.

For the next step is to ask the bowler to try a 'round-armer'. Check that he understands what round-arm means, and he will put his arm in the usual round-arm position, looking at you with that quizzical expression which means 'Do you really want me to bowl one down there? Who is this idiot?' Then he'll bowl one. Almost without exception such a bowler then bowls the ball in a perfect straight over the top position. And now you have the answer to the problem.

You see, when he thinks he is round-arm, he is straight over the top, and, thus logically, when he thinks he is straight over the top, he goes past the vertical. His mind has not grasped what the arm is doing – a not unusual occurrence.

So what next? If he is inaccurate all the time, the answer is for him to bowl what he thinks is round-arm all the time. If he is normally accurate, but, occasionally, the 'wheels fall off' and he begins to 'drop short' and stray down the leg, then the answer is to bowl a couple of 'round-armers'. This will usually get him back on line, settle him down, and then he can get back to bowling naturally and forgetting about all the previous hassles – until next time.

Usually, the past-the-vertical bowler does so naturally – he begins that way. And, as I have said before, if he can cope with it, let him go. But some of these bowling actions have been created by unintelligent coaching. From coaches who insist that bowlers must bowl 'high' with the arm 'scraping the ear'.

For any bowler such advice can be damaging if knowledge of his arm's position is vague. But for a wrist-spinner it can be disastrous.

Most leg-spinners have not bowled 'right over the top'. 'Cupping the ball over' from a half round-arm action allows greater use of 'all the levers' and maximizes spin. You do not have to go back to Grimmett to illustrate this; watch Shane Warne. Most wrist-spinners of average height or smaller have bowled that way.

Some of the taller men bowled very

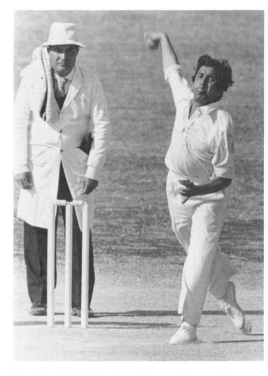

Fig 51   Abdul Qadir will not deliver this one from a very high position. He is slightly round-arm. For the leg-spinner there is little reason not to be. (Patrick Eagar)

high, and this did increase bounce for them even more. Benaud was a first-class example – he was high and obtained great bounce, but he was never a big turner. O'Reilly was high in the arm, but was, I repeat, unique.

The point is that there is no logical reason for a wrist-spinner to bowl with a high arm action. An off-spinner, yes. He must do so to obtain over-the-top-spin. If his arm is low, he must side-spin. But the wrist-spinner can spin over-the-top from a round-arm action. You try it! If anything, it can become more difficult over the top. 'Going

Figs 52–53 With exaggerated round-arm actions, the author spins over-the-top. One is a leg-spinner, the other a wrong'un. Which is which?

round the loop' is an easier exercise from the half round-arm position.

Furthermore, the little man will lose in another way from going unnecessarily high. From that position, he tends to create a more favourable line from hand to eye for the batsman, whereas from the cupped, half-round-arm position, the ball must go up first before it comes down, up above the batsman's eye level, and hence will maximize the batsman's problem of judging length.

To sum up. Personally, I would seldom encourage a wrist-spinner to lift his arm and bowl higher. To do so has no real value, and it can encourage an in-swing type action or even 'past-the-vertical'. Once again, let me clarify to avoid misunderstanding. I am not suggesting we should coach all leg-spinners to drop their arms down to a round-arm position. What I am saying is that there is nothing wrong with a semi-round-arm delivery for a leg-spinner, and that most smaller wrist-spinners have not been high at delivery. Thus we should not be insisting on a high arm action for all.

Furthermore, we must understand that by trying to get too high, many bowlers can go past the vertical with the consequent dangers of so doing. Most successful leg-spinners have had far more in common with the delivery of an out-swing bowler than an in-swing bowler.

THE FOLLOW THROUGH

In most ball games the action does not cease immediately when the ball is struck or released. A movement has begun and it should finish naturally.

Fig 54   Qadir explodes through the crease into his follow through. It is the follow through of a real spin bowler not a slow bowler. (Patrick Eagar)

That is part of the rhythm involved.

Thus, after the ball is released, the bowler's body continues its movement. If the bowler has exploded through the crease, as he should, that movement will be quite substantial. The back leg will pivot around the braced front leg, and the momentum will carry the bowler's body on for several yards at least.

If the bowler does not follow through naturally several yards, he is either forcing himself to stop – which is unnatural and jerky – or he did not have enough 'oomph' in his approach and delivery in the first place. The

Fig 55 Shane Warne has really given the ball a flick, exploded through the crease, and followed through. But there is still a relaxed, balanced rhythm to it all. (Patrick Eagar)

latter is usually the cause of lack of follow through. If there is something wrong, carefully examine approach and delivery, and adjust what may be necessary there. For to simply 'tack on' a follow through will be as much use in the long-term as an aspirin for a toothache.

Summing Up Accuracy

With most bowlers, when the necessary work on concentration is done, particularly as self-confidence grows, accuracy will improve rapidly

and dramatically. Great changes to approach, delivery and follow through will seldom be necessary.

If changes are necessary they will seldom be major and you will probably need an observer to watch you. But get on with them quickly at practice, work at them until they become natural and automatic, and never introduce the change into a match situation until it is natural and automatic. You must not be thinking about your action as you bowl in a match. This is certain disaster!

And for the coach. If change is essential, help him get on with it at practice. Do all you can to get it out of his mind in matches until he is fully comfortable with it.

And most importantly! If a bowler has been inaccurate and you are working with him to help him, it is probable that someone or even the bowler himself, has suspected that his action is at fault. It is possible that he has been watching his action carefully. When you feel assured that the action is not the cause of inaccuracy – and it usually is not – *make sure you clarify this to the bowler.* Assure him that he can forget his run up, delivery and follow through and simply bowl. His action is **not** causing the trouble.

This is important because whilst he thinks about his action as he bowls, he has lost concentration. He is thinking about things he should not be thinking about and that itself is the most common cause of inaccuracy. So much so that the simple assurance that the action is all clear, and should be put altogether out of the bowler's mind, is often enough to bring about the improvement in accuracy sought after. For you have solved a cause of semi-concentration.

3. POWER

'Power' is not a word you hear much about in spin-bowling. With the 'quicks', yes, but seldom the spinners. Yet for spinners it should be just as important. It is more obvious with the pacemen. They apply their power behind the centre of the ball, and it results in pace. That is easy to understand. It is also easy to understand that it is not only the fingers doing the final work behind the ball, which have created that pace. It is a product of the approach and delivery, the rhythm and timing, and the explosive effort of both arms and body through the crease at delivery.

All this is true of the spinner, but it is not as easily seen or understandable. As I have said before, you must be a 'spin-bowler' not a 'slow-bowler'. The emphasis must be on 'spin' not 'slowness of pace'.

The spin-bowler should be applying all the same bases of power on the ball as the paceman. But whereas the paceman puts this power behind *the centre* of the ball for pace, the spinner puts it on *one side* for spin. Naturally then it does not come out of the hand as fast as the pace man, but just as much effort has been involved, and usually the final explosion of effort through the crease at delivery is just as great. Watch Shane Warne at delivery.

This goes back to what I stressed in the section on 'Eight Stages of Spin'. All the levers (fingers, wrist, forearm,

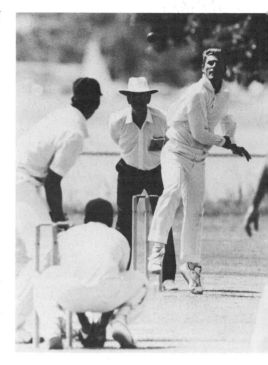

Fig 56   Young Western Australian leg-spinner Stuart McGill really gives the ball a flick with fingers and wrist, but the body has not been fully involved. This is shown by his remaining in the upright position in the follow through.

elbow and shoulder) must be fully involved in spinning the ball, but so must both arms and the whole body. The uplifted front arm bearing body weight back, the transference of weight from back to forward, the forward rotation of shoulders, the drive forward of the body, the tucked in front arm to retain side-on position, the powerful pivot around a braced front leg which causes a strong follow through, the fact that after delivery the bowling shoulder now faces the batsman – all these are the indications of the power that any quality spinner

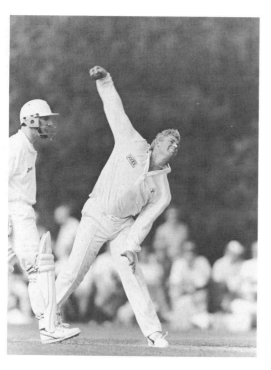

Fig 57 Despite the relaxation, 'all the levers' are working on the ball. The effort is total. He is exploding. (Patrick Eagar)

Fig 58 Kerry O'Keefe has certainly exploded through the crease and illustrated the power that quality spinners put into their delivery.

is putting on the ball as he *explodes through the crease*. No wonder so many of them grunt or half-grunt with the effort involved at that moment. Why should slow bowlers grunt?

I emphasize 'power' in this book for the very reason that it is seldom heard in discussing spin-bowling. That is probably why too many spinners, particularly youngsters, bowl with only one arm, with little body drive (or 'power') and a negligible follow through. They simply do not understand what real spin is and what it demands. They are slow-bowlers not spin-bowlers, and they have little future in the game.

Obviously 'power' is linked with 'spin' and it is also linked with 'pace'. I have already briefly mentioned the problem of what pace to bowl in Chapter 3 and I shall pursue it again, and in greater depth, in Chapter 6.

Don't forget that word 'power', will you? On occasions when you bowl in the nets take the opportunity to half close your eyes and feel, and visualize, the working of 'all the levers' and the 'power' of the body and action in creating spin.

4. VARIATIONS

It is important to keep variation in perspective. Small and subtle variations combined with accuracy, experience and thought can create an outstanding bowler. It is not necessary to have 'the whole box of tricks' and use them constantly. It is fair to say that 'accuracy without variation limits you, but variation without accuracy is nothing'.

In wrist-spin, because so many dramatic variations are available, it is easy to overlook the simple, minor variations.

Minor Variations

These are pace, angle and line. Their advantage is that because so little change is necessary they should never affect accuracy.

Variation of pace should be basic. You have your normal pace, your 'bread and butter' pace, which makes up the majority of your deliveries. You can then bowl some balls slightly faster, and others slightly slower. Now you have three paces. The best change of pace is slight, so slight that the batsman is only aware of it after he has played it, and looks up and smiles – if he has survived. For such changes of pace, there is no real need for changing grips etc., it is simply a matter of normal effort, a little more, or a little less.

In modern 'limited overs cricket', dramatic slower balls have come into vogue. The half-ball grip, the leg-spin type, off-spin type and many others have been introduced to create a delivery noticeably slower than its predecessor. They are particularly successful later in an innings when batsmen are charging or slogging.

But in 'normal cricket' situations, such a dramatically slower ball is easily identified, and the sensible batsman simply plays forward, kills it, and awaits the next. As I have said, the subtly slower or faster ball is not so easily identified or dealt with. For the wrist-spinner that dramatically slower ball is hardly relevant anyway. But the inter-mixture of subtle changes of pace is basic and never-ending.

A couple of warnings. When you are trying to bowl a faster ball, don't leave it all to a final 'oomph' at delivery. A likely result of that is that you will drop short. Better to speed up the approach fractionally to lead into the increase of power at delivery. If it is subtly done, it is not necessarily obvious.

And with the slower ball. The danger is that we are likely to lob it up with less spin on it. The secret must be to spin it just as hard, probably with over-spin, to help it come down quicker. That will take a lot of practice.

And lastly! You will always vary your pace, but when you do achieve the skills of 'going around the loop' (that is, 'over the top', 'around the side' and 'underneath') they will often do that work for you. 'Over the top' will give you the advantages of the slower ball, and 'underneath' the advantages of the quicker ball, whilst 'round the side' will add another complication. Your changes of pace then come from what your hand is doing.

Angle variation is another simple but effective ploy. Most leg-spinners

Line variation. On most occasions, wrist-spinners will settle into a particular line of attack for different batsmen and conditions. For instance, on a good wicket to most right-hand batsmen he may try to work along middle and off-stump line. I shall discuss 'line' in more detail in Chapter 6.

What I am looking at here, however, is the tactical use of changing line, something of great importance to a wrist-spinner, for one of his most useful tactics is to 'widen' on a batsman. This means plugging away on off-stump, getting the batsman forward and wanting to drive you. Then, occasionally throwing up the ball a little further, *but wider*, preferably with a little more over-spin on it.

Quite clearly, a ball pitched a foot outside off-stump, even though it is on the same length as one pitched on middle-stump, is further away from the batsman. The 'widening' then is another, but more subtle, way of shortening the length of a delivery. The wrist-spinner thus hopes to catch the batsman playing short of the pitch of the ball with consequent chances of stumping and catches behind, in the slips or in the in-field.

As I have said an intelligent bowler who combines a stock delivery, such as a leg-break, with accuracy and these simple minor variations of pace, angle and line can be very successful indeed. But, inevitably, if he is a true wrist-spinner at heart, he will become fascinated by the more dramatic variations which are available to him.

Major Variations

These are, of course, the variations

Fig 59   Bob Holland has gone out wide on the crease for this one. Beware not to bowl it more like an in-swinger than an out-swinger. (Patrick Eagar)

should try to bowl in close to the stumps. If you can get in there for your stock ball, and so bowl up along the line of the stumps, you can always go out wide when you want to. But get into the habit of bowling from wide out, and it can become very difficult indeed to 'get in close'.

So by bowling some wide on the crease, and others close in, we have a simple variation of angle. But don't become too clever by having half-a-dozen positions along the crease, and thus, in theory, six different angles. That will upset you, the bowler, far more than it will the batsman.

available to the wrist-spinner, caused by spin, in

* Turn.
* Drop.
* Bounce.
* Drift.
* Skid.
* Varying trajectories.
* Varying lengths.

If I am not careful, I shall become excited about this magic again, and repeat it. But it has all been set out in Chapter 3, the 'Eight Stages of Spin', particularly in that wonderful exercise of 'going around the loop'. Whether you remember those sections perfectly or not, I suggest you skim through them again now anyway.

A final comment. It is natural for a real wrist-spinner to be absorbed in these major variations, even to seek more. It is good that he should try to understand and master all of them, and an advantage if he can add them to his practical repertoire and use them at will. But there have been plenty of fine wrist-spinners who did not have them all. There have been plenty with limited resources, who have used them craftily in association with accuracy and guile.

Remember that though 'accuracy without variation is limiting, variation without accuracy is nothing'. Don't be one of those 'Heinz bowlers' – the ones with fifty-seven varieties – who constantly go through their repertoire and bowl a bag of garbage.

Variation should be sensible. Remember that until you establish a stock ball variation is pointless. Remember too, that you need to accumulate pressure on batsmen to win your bowling victories and you cannot build such pressure by consistently letting him off the hook through inaccuracy. Trying to bowl too much too often, trying too hard, is a sure way to do that.

Nevertheless, I have no doubt that the wrist-spinner who can master and control all the variations, then introduce them with accuracy and subtlety as required, can only be a better bowler. In 1994 in England, I watched Shane Warne literally 'go around the loop' in the Test matches. It was like a practice session as he whizzed through the variations, and it left the English batsmen in awe, bewilderment and admiration. A young wrist-spinner should not require motivation to interest him in the major variations, but if he did, the example of Shane Warne should be enough.

5. EXPERIENCE, KNOWLEDGE, TACTICS

Of course, I cannot simply write down all you need to know about these. They must take time and often only by going through something and doing it will you fully understand. Nevertheless, there are many short-cuts, ways to learn and things to store away, which can be achieved earlier than simply waiting for them to happen (*see* Chapter 7, 'Advanced Tactics').

Many of us have had to learn these the hard way. I had no one to explain most of what I am talking to you about; I had to work it out for myself. Perhaps it was a wonderful intellectual exercise and good for my soul. But, boy, it wasted some years – years when, had I already possessed the knowledge, I could have been making good use of it. *So the value of coaching and education is to find out things earlier than you would normally.* Too many bowlers only discover knowledge of value as their playing careers end. Sounds like 'life' again!

Right through this book, I am throwing information at you. As the old-time teachers used to say, 'If you throw enough mud at the wall, some will stick.' I hope you are collecting some 'mud' here and there.

Books can help, regardless of what some will say to the contrary. But they cannot do it all. You must expect to learn, and build your knowledge and understanding, every match you play, every practice you attend, every game you watch. You can always learn in this game. You never know it all. Often that is harder to accept when you are younger, but, believe me, it is true. So think carefully about the game always. Use your mind and your body. Look at pitches carefully; remember what they do. Think of winds you come across, and their effect, learn from different weather conditions.

Watch each batsman – and bowler – you come across. Watch carefully. Analyse. What are the strengths, the weaknesses? What would be the best way to attack, or defend, to him? At matches, or on television, spend time simply watching the batsman (or the bowler, or the wicket-keeper) rather than watching the cricket. Just stare at the individual player and everything he does for half an hour. Do the same in the nets.

If you come across a new player – batsmen or bowler – find time to have a good look at him. This is particularly so if he is a little different. For instance a wrist-spinner with a good flipper or googly. Make it part of your personal pride to work him out, never allow anyone to possess something different that puzzles you. Part of that is, of course, understanding whatever can happen in theory. Once you understand that, recognizing it in practice is far easier. Far too many cricketers, modern batsmen in particular, do not understand how or why things happen in theory, and are lost when it confronts them in practice. Don't let yourself fall into that category. Be inquisitive. Try to find out 'why'. Try to understand 'how'. A good start to that is by reading this book carefully.

So, an important part of your career is to accumulate cricket knowledge. As a wrist-spinner much of this should be about wrist-spin, but, as a successful wrist-spinner, you must understand batting, wicket-keeping and fielding. *You must.*

Too many cricketers do not try to accumulate knowledge to understand. Or they do not try hard enough to do so. Many simply play in a blissful haze of happy non-understanding. That is fair enough if they are satisfied with mediocrity, but it is unacceptable if they wish to excel, to do their very best, to use talent to its optimum. Nor is it a chore. Involving yourself totally in the game, both mentally and physically, and wrestling with its problems and intricacies is what attracts so many people to cricket. It is a complex game, a thought-provoking game, a worthwhile way of life.

Finally, it is an oversimplification to believe that all cricketers will become experienced with time. It is not so. Many young players can be experienced; many older players are never so. For to be 'experienced' demands that you accumulate knowledge and *learn from it*. Experienced players do not keep on making the same mistake time after time.

There are very many cricketers who have been playing for a lifetime who are not 'experienced players'. They are simply 'old players'. There is a world of difference.

So build up your knowledge and, hopefully, experience. You will come to recognize weaknesses and strengths, and accumulate skills and tactics to deal with them. It is one thing to recognize the weakness and understand the necessary tactic to attack it, it is another to be able to master the necessary delivery and bowl it where required. Similarly, it is one thing to have the ability to both bowl the necessary delivery and control it, and quite another to recognize the weakness and the required tactic.

Thus, in the long run, the successful bowler is the one who has achieved all those ingredients referred to in this chapter. His attitude was right to get this far. He worked conscientiously and intelligently to achieve accuracy. He spun hard, giving the ball a flick, and developed power in his delivery. He gradually acquired the necessary variations both minor and major and controlled them. Accumulated knowledge and experience enabled him to develop tactics to best use his array of skills in attacking each individual batsman who confronted him.

That is successful bowling – successful wrist-spin bowling. Easy, isn't it?

CHAPTER 5

Mind and Body

THE BODY

We live in a cricketing age when the 'physical' is emphasized more than ever before. Emphasis on biomechanics; on fitness, strength and stamina via the gymnasium and the weight-room; on the importance of flexibility and a thousand different stretching exercises; on dieting, liquid intake and lifestyle – these constitute an almost entirely new dimension in cricket.

Of course they are very important, for all these physical matters can significantly improve performance. But there is also little doubt that they can be over-emphasized and misused in cricket preparation. Of this we must all be very wary. Increased awareness of the value of physical training in cricket can only be an improvement, but it must be kept in perspective. Fitness and strength should never be allowed to replace, or even interfere with, the development of skills.

That may sound old-fashioned, but it is certainly not meant to be. I admire much of what is done in modern fitness techniques and programmes, though I still believe that much more of the most meaningful fitness work should be done by bowling, fielding and batting more. When Sir Donald Bradman was questioned about his own early season fitness programmes,

Fig 60   Modern warm-up and stretching exercises before practice and matches. A tough task-master, Dennis Ward has worked the West Indies in this phase for many years, and the value of his work speaks for itself. (Patrick Eagar)

he replied that he made sure he got an early season double century. There is much wisdom there, for the best way to get fit for batting is to bat.

But we must not be unreasonable. First of all, Sir Don was good enough to almost ensure an early season double hundred and consequent batting fitness. Most of us are not. Secondly, Sir Don grew up in different times with a totally different lifestyle. Particularly as a country boy, he grew up in a world with far different expectations, means of transport, food supply and comparative affluence – so many things, many of which were for his physical betterment.

We must accept that many things in society have changed. One is that young people are less naturally fit. They do little walking, and almost no running, as part of their everyday normal life. Previous generations grew up either walking or running everywhere; if not, they simply stayed at home. There was not the car transportation; no money for public transportation. So they walked, or they ran, as the usual means of transportation from age two to fifteen. This certainly built a base of natural fitness.

This is certainly not the case for the majority today. In a complicated world, children are transported by private car to most places, because of fear, laziness or fashion. As they grow up, they buy their own cars. To go half a mile down the street they drive, with seldom a thought of walking. That is not meant as a criticism, it is a statement of fact.

Furthermore, they are surrounded by an array of foodstuffs, most of it pushed at them by constant advertising, and they have the means to purchase it in most cases. This makes them the most over-fed generation in history. The easy availability of such vast varieties of food is apparent at once on any walk through a modern supermarket.

The combination of lack of natural exercise and excess food availability creates the easy possibility of very unfit young people. When added to this that the most easily accessible forms of exercise for young people – backyard and street games plus school sport – have virtually disappeared from the modern scene, the dangers of lack of fitness to a degree of serious public health problems for young people are very real. It is a major social problem for the future, far greater than the comparative examination results of schools. Of course, this book deals with sportsmen, so the final glum conclusion doesn't apply to them. They are at least playing sport. But the other realities of modern life are still there for them too – the lack of early natural exercise, the temptations and probability of excess and incorrect food intake.

From my observations over thirty-five years of teaching, and a similar time in coaching youth sport, I have no doubt that modern youth is less fit naturally. Many catch up through the use of the gymnasium, weights and other training programmes, but what is done artificially may be different in some ways to what was formerly done naturally almost from toddler to teenager.

Certain incidents in Adelaide whilst

I was the South Australian coach convinced me of this. In particular, I recall fitness tests run at the end of a playing season, then repeated several months later after the season had ended. Some of the results shocked me. Several young players, top sportsmen less than twenty years old, had deteriorated physically to an appalling extent in this short space of time. They were not slobs. They were talented, decent, normal lads on the verge of first-class cricket. Yet one had put on almost a stone in weight in that time, with all the expected associated losses of fitness and flexibility. Virtually all had declined noticeably.

That would not have happened years ago. Firstly, most of them, as talented games players, would have been playing a winter sport such as one of the football codes, hockey or baseball. But, of course, the demands of modern sport from an early age will not allow a two-sport year. A great shame, I believe! In addition, their normal life would have involved much walking and running. And, I repeat, the temptation and ready availability of vast quantities of food would not have been there.

Yes, society has changed and therefore so have needs. Today, modern young cricketers do need fitness training on a scale never contemplated in previous years. But what old-timers should understand is that though some of the fitness training can become obsessive and out of perspective, much of it is only a catching-up process. They need it to compensate for what they would have obtained naturally in previous years.

To wrist-spin bowlers I offer this advice. The most important part of fitness you require – the strength, the stamina and flexibility – will come *if you bowl enough*. That means at least six hours a week over years and years. Added to that should be a sensible lifestyle, which includes the normal walking and running your legs are meant to do, plus sensible eating, drinking and sleeping. Also, I strongly believe that you should be playing another off-season sport during winter.

These, coupled with the other cricket training and practice, which involves batting, fielding and general activity, are enough. If you do all of this, then long distance running, the gym work and all the other fitness programmes are non-essentials. If they interest you, by all means get stuck in, for it is unlikely that you can get too fit. But if you are one of the many modern youths who do not practise enough, do not live a sensible lifestyle, do not have a winter sport, and generally under-perform physically, then a fitness programme will be necessary for you.

For a wrist-spinner there is one part of the body, however, which needs particular attention – the fingers of the bowling hand. Every spinner who gives the ball a flick – and that means most of them who want to be any good – will suffer finger damage at times. But it is best to try to avoid it.

In the past, various solutions have been suggested to anoint the spinning fingers pre-season and early season to toughen them. Friars balsam and methylated spirits were long used, though the toughened calluses so created tend to flake off, leaving soft flesh. Urinating on the fingers was an old, less sophisticated ploy, which does not appeal to everyone. Since the days of Richie Benaud another chemical method has spread. From the pharmacy, calamine oleosa, an oily, creamy liquid, was purchased and rubbed into the spinning fingers then coated with boracic acid powder. I used to do this for hours on the train going off to work over many years and it did form a tough pad which did not crack or flake. It worked.

But perhaps even more important, is sensible treatment of the fingers early in the season in particular, and common sense throughout. Start spinning gradually at home in the off-season. You don't need a pitch, a batting opponent, just a ball. Just chalk up spinning hours, never using a ball with a new hard potentially cutting seam. Then move into a twenty-two yard situation somewhere for a couple of weeks before you attend the early season official practices. Again choose your ball carefully. Nothing too hard or abrasive. Of course, you will want to impress at those early season official practices and/or matches and part of that is to bowl as much as possible to show off your wares. But, again, where possible build up gradually and choose your ball carefully.

It becomes clear here that you should be carrying your own ball around to practise with. Within reason, this is true. Have a ball which is twenty or thirty overs old, still hard with a decent seam and some shine – a realistic match ball, that is – but not with the up-raised, razor seams that

some new balls have. That is looking for early season trouble. Of course, it is necessary to bowl with all sorts of balls at practice. You don't wish to develop a ball-obsession that some bowlers do when they come to feel that they cannot bowl unless the ball is right. You must be confident you can bowl with 'anything'. But have a couple of tried and trusted safe ones tucked away in the kit. Just in case!

That is all I wish to say about the formal fitness programme here. I am NOT against them, but there are many far more qualified than I to discuss them. I simply say again, don't get the physical part of the game out of perspective. Of course, you must be fit, but that part of the game must never outweigh skills. And, even more important than the physical or the skills, is the mind.

THE MIND

The mind determines and controls everything; all skills, all things physical. You can have all the skills, all the talent in the world, all the strength, stamina and flexibility – but without the mind to look after it all, the result is nil.

By no means does this mean that you must be a mental giant. All human beings are intelligent. But what is essential is to control your mind, to educate and discipline it in certain areas.

I have listened to many lectures from sports psychologists. All were thoroughly worth while and the best left me with the lasting impression that most of what they said was thoughtful common sense rather than mumbo-jumbo. That is usually a good sign. My other impression was that the conclusions they reached, often from the academic end, usually coincided with those I had formulated personally over time from the practical playing end. Let me make it clear that what I discuss in the following pages is the latter – my conclusions reached from a lifetime of playing, coaching cricket and rugby, teaching, living, and, most important, bowling wrist-spin.

'Buts and Ifs'

We have all played with or against, met or heard of, talented players 'who had it all', but 'never quite made it'. They were better than so and so the Test player BUT . . . They could have been great players IF . . .

Almost without exception, such a player has not made it because of mental limitations. That doesn't mean he was stupid. It could have been because he lacked motivation – it simply did not mean enough to him, or he did not believe in himself. Or he could have lacked concentration skills, or self-confidence. Perhaps it was his inability to manage the inevitable stress involved, or that his approach to the game was out of perspective. Perhaps he tried too hard, found it difficult to relax and was too hard on himself in his search for excellence.

All of these things are 'of the mind'. There are many others, too, which are entirely mental. More cricketers have failed or succeeded because of these, than because of matters relating to

skills, talent and fitness combined. The road of first-class cricket, in particular, is littered with the casualties whose failure was in the mind. Similarly, many a player of limited ability has reached the top because of his strength of mind.

There is simply no point in discussing cricketers who were good enough BUT. . . . In cricket, as in life, there are no 'ifs' and there are no 'buts'. You either do or you don't, you make it or you don't. The reasons and excuses, in the long run, are quite meaningless – irrelevant.

For those who wish to 'make it', it is important right from the start to accept that, more often than not, how your mind works will be the most important single deciding factor. And, just as you can develop your physical fitness, hone your skills, build your cricket knowledge and experience, and more fully utilize your *natural ability*, so there is much you can learn to help you in your mental approach to cricket in general, and wrist-spinning in particular.

Motivation

I am not here to talk you into being a great wrist-spinner, a good wrist-spinner, a fair wrist-spinner, or an enthusiastic but relatively unskilled wrist-spinner. I am assuming that you want to be a wrist-spinner – very much – and that I am simply offering you help to achieve that goal.

So my purpose is not to sell wrist-spin to the disinterested or the undeserving. But if your desire is there, regardless of your talent, skill or physique, I want to help you. And the first thing I can do is to refer you back to Chapter 4, and the section on 'Attitude'. Because 'desire' is what it is all about. If you want it enough, if wanting to be a wrist-spinner means enough to you to do the thinking and the working required, you will get there.

Certainly how far you go will relate to your natural ability and physical qualities, but your *motivation* can compensate for a great deal of limitations in those departments. Not all Test cricketers are great players. They never have been. Most are talented players who worked at it.

If you have reasonable natural talent, you have fair ball sense, you find spinning the ball natural, you are a reasonable ball games player – and you love cricket, particularly wrist-spinning – then 'go for it'. The sky is the limit for you. You can achieve whatever you are prepared to work for.

When I was a youngster, I used to watch first-grade cricket in Sydney and regard the players out on the field as supermen whom I could never hope to emulate. When I reached first-grade, I viewed the New South Wales Sheffield Shield players in a similar light, then having achieved State cricket, the Test scene seemed equally distant and unattainable. But I worked and it came.

Only then did I come to realize that there are few giants at the top. There are very few geniuses and only a handful of greats. Most are like you – and me – with reasonable talent, a capacity to work and think, and a great driving desire to enjoy wrist-spinning and to do it as well as pos-

Fig 61 Garfield Sobers was a genius. Here he bowls his seamers from wide on the crease. He also bowled world-class wrist-spinners with the same perfect action. (Patrick Eagar)

sible. Rest assured, that is enough to get you on the way. Be confident that with that attitude and work ethic, you can achieve anything. Go for it! Do your very best! Climb to the levels of cricket you want! And enjoy every moment of it!

Preparation

When you sit for an examination, perform in a play or musical concert, give a speech, or compete in any sporting event, it is not simply your thoughts and actions during the event itself that determine the success of your performance. In cricket, *every match is an examination* in its own way, which will measure not only your natural ability, application, determination, concentration and temperament, but what you have learnt and stored away over the preceding years of your career, what your pre-match preparation was like, as well as the quality of the match effort itself.

In the long run, each of us should be satisfied if the result – the match day performance – is what we deserve based on the combination of the above factors.

We all know that there are many people who have false expectations. Though they have done little long-term practice, have not accumulated know-how, have neglected correct practice methods over the last months, weeks and days before the match, have ignored the importance of the mind and body immediately before the match, or may even have very limited ability, they expect glamorous results.

Such people are deluding themselves, and here I am not concerned with them. The world is all too full of those who expect maximum returns with the minimum input and effort, and they already receive too much sympathy. I am greatly concerned however with the many who have reasonable talent, have worked hard over the years, have done 'the right thing' as they see it, yet collect disappointing performances – performances that are not commensurate with their ability, effort and preparation. *Almost certainly, in such cases, the problem is in the mind*, and can be helped by a little bit of common sense and understanding. So let me say a few words about preparation.

LONG-TERM PREPARATION
This means all those years you have played the game. If you have had sound practice methods over those years, you have worked hard and intelligently, you have accumulated technique, knowledge and experience, these will always stand by you. They will always be there to give you that background security and confidence which is a solid and sensible base upon which to build anything. Such an awareness is a warm reassurance before even the most demanding of contests.

If you do not have this background, you are unlikely to catch it up. Nor is there anything you can do about it on the eve of a match, so your best strategy is to ignore it completely. For it is beyond your control and you should never waste time or energy on matters which are not under your control.

MEDIUM-TERM PREPARATION
By medium term, I refer to what has happened so far during the current season. And, generally, the same applies to what has been said above about long-term preparation. If you have done it well, it will bring its rewards; if you have not, you will suffer for that because you deserve to, but there is no point dwelling on that limitation.

An important proviso! If you are in the midst of a season, when you have not been getting 'a good bowl' in matches – which can happen all too often with wrist-spinners these days –

you must increase your practice. That sounds logical, but often the tendency is to do just the opposite. Because we are not getting the overs we would like, or feel we deserve, we bowl less at practice whether in disappointment, frustration, anger or despair. We must of course bowl more, using any or all of the different methods of spin practice outlined in the early chapters of this book to compensate for the lack of match play.

We must do this, so that we are as well prepared as possible for that moment, when the captain says one day, 'Hey, Pete. Have a bowl. We need you'. If we have continued to practise hard, we are now able to maximize the opportunity knowing that if we do perform, we shall earn the opportunity more often in the future. Too often, however, the opposite happens. You lack match play, you have reduced practice, you at last given the opportunity, and you are poorly prepared. Now you are less likely to perform well, and you reduce the likelihood of future opportunities.

SHORT-TERM PREPARATION
This refers to the days before the match, the night before and the morning before. To perform as well as you deserve in each contest – which means showing off your long-term and short-term preparation plus your natural ability and all your acquired knowledge, skills and experience – depends very much on this short-term preparation.

On the day, you want your body and mind *fit and relaxed* so that what you have to offer can come out uninterrupted. So what you eat, what you drink, and how you sleep are vital. For most of us, that does not mean some complicated diet. It should mean eating, drinking and sleeping as you normally do in following your normal lifestyle. As you go up the ladder of cricket this can be difficult. Often you are living in up-market hotels surrounded by temptations. Try to live with them and utilize them sensibly.

Don't go off to bed far earlier than usual. Your mind is then likely to keep you awake all night. Don't have late nights which will drain you. If you normally have a few beers, have them. But don't have a binge. Eat sensibly, normally. Stick to your normal way of life. This all sounds common sense and it is. But it is so often ignored, and then the body and mind which take the field are not in their best relaxed, energetic state to show off fully their long accumulated talents.

If you are the type who gets 'uptight', find ways to relax: the movies, TV, reading, swimming, chatting with friends. For many, it is better to avoid talking cricket. The last thing you want is an over-stimulated mind that refuses to allow a tired body to sleep. Get to know yourself and avoid things that leave you less than best for the following day.

When the morning of the match arrives be sensible again. We want that mind and body on the field most likely to perform at their best. Don't leave things to the last moment, and get yourself hassled. Check kit and transport the night before. Make sure your transport is under your own control. If not, double check it!

Don't arrive too early at the ground for you. Nor too late for you. Learn the final procedure at the ground before the match which is best for you. If you have a coach, he should be sensible enough to allow you individuality in your morning's pre-match preparation. Read what follows on stress management, and, above all, keep in mind that no matter how ambitious you may be, the primary reason that you are going out to play cricket is *to enjoy it*. Never forget that – enjoy it. It will help you to relax and so to perform.

YOU ARE ABOUT TO BOWL

The moment comes. You have been brought into the attack. By now you should have checked wind directions, and hopefully persuaded the captain to give you the end you want. If not, forget it, for it is better to bowl from the wrong end, than not bowl at all.

As for field placements, you should have worked these out well in advance with the captain. You should know what you want, what he will allow you, and what any compromise will be. This must be settled well in advance, for you certainly don't want this worry now.

You are on to bowl with the field you expected and, if possible, the wind as you wanted it. The rest is up to you, to show off all that accumulated effort over the years to the very best of your ability.

First, always *build your bowling* as a batsman should build his innings. Just as he does not set out to smash every ball in the early overs if he wishes to stay in, you do not try to bowl every variety you have, or try to bowl each batsman out every ball if you wish to stay on. Just settle down.

You can expect to bowl thirty overs today, so take your time. Even if the captain throws you the ball two overs before a break in play, do the same. Don't try too hard. Relax and enjoy your craft.

For most of us, early on it is better to bowl *slightly* slower. It will help relax you, and the ball is more likely to be 'up there'. The last thing we want early is to be 'short'. Hurry, tension, and above-normal speed, can cause that. So relax, bowl fractionally slower, run up rhythmically into your delivery, spin hard and get the ball well up on your chosen line. Whatever that line may be (*see* Chapter 6), the field set should be appropriate for it. If you keep the ball up, spinning hard, on that line, with the field backing you, not too much can go wrong as you settle down. Don't be too ambitious, just concentrate on the simple things as yet, don't try too hard, and let it happen. 'The Circle of Concentration' (*see* the part of this section on 'Concentration') can be a very helpful aid at this stage.

What has been said above can help you to settle down in your early overs. We all need that. Then, gradually, you can begin to develop your attack and show off your wares.

THE GAME IS OVER

Post-match assessment hardly seems like preparation. But it is, for there is always a next match. In assessing your performance, you should accept the concept that you should be satisfied with what you deserve. That was the point of this discussion on preparation. You did not wish to waste those years of practice, your preparation this season, your care over the last week, your natural ability, knowledge and experience. You wanted to obtain returns commensurate to the combination of the above factors.

That certainly does not mean that you sell yourself short and settle for mediocrity. Not at all. If you want to be as good as you can be, you must stretch yourself, seek excellence, demand one hundred per cent input, and expect an equal return. Your expectations should be high, but *real*. If you come to think this way, then you will reach that ultimate mental position where you gain your satisfaction from doing your best, giving a hundred per cent and performing to the best of your ability. After all, you can do no more than that.

Instead of an obsession with results (how many wickets you take) you become obsessed with *performance* (how well you bowl). If you bowl well, as well as you should do, you are happy and have obtained a personal victory. Results are a pleasant bonus to be tacked on to a good performance, not vice versa. The earlier you reach this state of mind, the more fortunate you are, as it decreases unnecessary worry and strain. For, if you continue to bowl well, concerning yourself with this rather than how many wickets you get, you must succeed eventually. If you keep bowling well, wickets must come. But, if you are satisfied with wickets, even though you are not bowling well, that cannot last.

In the long run, you have control only over how you bowl, that is your performance. You do not have control over how many wickets you get, for

there are so many variables which will determine that, and most of them are beyond your control.

The ultimate lesson to learn in your bowling is to concentrate on those things over which you **do** have control and try to get out of your mind altogether those matters over which you have no control. That is what is meant by concentrating on performance rather than results** (*see* 'Circle of Concentration' below in the part of this section on concentration). This is obvious when you consider it, but it can take a lot of learning. Many never do learn it, and it remains an unnecessary complication for them.

To summarize. Every time we perform in a match, we want a performance deserving of the long-term and medium-term preparation we have put in, combined with our natural ability, knowledge and experience. The short-term preparation helps to ensure that. If we obtain the performance we deserve, in the light of these things, we are satisfied.

Stress Management and Relaxation

'Stress' is a misunderstood word. That misunderstanding alone, the belief that stress is in itself a negative force, can create 'over-stress', which is a negative force. Stress is natural for all human beings. It is not only natural, but a positive stimulus for improved performance.

Any human being at a nil stress level is as totally relaxed as possible, for instance asleep. At such a stage, few human beings are able to perform physically or mentally to the best of their ability. As relaxation decreases, stress increases. As you are confronted by the inevitable problems of each day and the necessary decision-making increases, you become more 'stressed'. In a state of controlled stress you are better able to make these decisions and, if physical action is required, controlled stress also helps you to perform better.

This has always been so of human beings. When the caveman left his cave and was confronted by some terrifying beast, he knew what 'stress' was. And it was the stress that gave him the additional strength to run faster or swing his club harder, which, perhaps, saved him. When you are driving a car and meet a sudden

emergency, it can be the faster reaction and thinking created by stress which can save you. In an exam, controlled stress can help to facilitate and accelerate your decision-making – and save you again! But – and this is the key – it is 'controlled stress'. Look at the diagram.

For all of us, there is an area where stress reaches *an optimum stage where we function best physically and mentally.* Few function very well at very low stress levels. We are too relaxed and need some pepping up. A little more excitement, tension and a little less relaxation and eventually we move into our area of optimum stress and relaxation, where we perform best. Such a level is difficult to

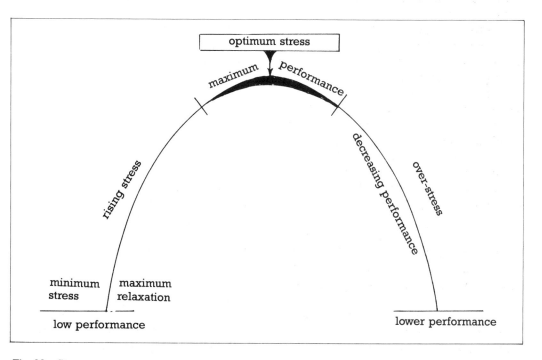

Fig 62   Stress curve.

measure, it is different for each individual, but most of us recognize it. We recognize when we are flat, just not 'revving up', under-stressed. We feel the mind begin to 'rev' and the blood start to churn, as we move towards the optimum stage. We are starting to 'tick over'.

And, without doubt, all of us, too, can remember the warning signs as we move into the danger zone, the stage of over-stress. With this can come physical symptoms such as an uneasy stomach – butterflies, even nausea; excessive heat or cold; blushing or paleness; sweat; trembling hands. Mentally, we can become confused, forgetful, hassled, generally uncomfortable with ourselves and others. At this stage, physical and/or mental performance decreases in efficiency. You are likely to freeze or be over-excited – perhaps you find it difficult to move quickly, remember, or think and act quickly or efficiently. Most of us have encountered something like this, and always at some moment of importance – an exam, a speech, a play, a match, a proposal! We have moved into over-stress, and the solution to it is logical.

To get out of the over-stress zone, we need increased relaxation. For most, this will take some time, but, for the sportsman, the politician, the actor, the musician, or the would-be lover, it is preferable to have remedies available, well tried and immediate. We shall examine some of these remedies in a moment.

But first let us examine the consequences of what has been said above. Few serious cricketers (and, of course, that includes all wrist-

Fig 63   Even the biggest, toughest and most determined can feel exhaustion and stress. Few have been tougher than Merv Hughes. (Patrick Eagar)

spinners!) are ever likely to be in the zone of under-stress before or during a match. It means too much to them. Most of them will be in the zone of optimum stress, we hope, but many are likely to be on the verge of, or well into, over-stress.

Each requires individual help rather than group therapy, which reveals the nonsense of the old-fashioned coaching 'psyche-up'. For to raise the excitement level – or stress levels – of players already in the over-stress zone

Fig 64   Relaxation becomes essential.
Dennis Lillee begins to relax after a hard
day in the field. (Milton Wordley)

could, though it was often too late. They had relaxed back out of the over-stress stage.

Pre-match motivation must only be an individual thing. Few need hyping up; most need leaving alone; and many need calming down and relaxing. That is why over-formalized warm-ups on the day of the match make little sense, and are often more for appearances and the benefit of the coach than the players.

The higher we go in sport, the greater the stress levels. The more it means to the individual, the greater the stress levels. How many batsmen have got out early in their innings because of uncontrolled stress? How many bowlers have under-performed early for the same reason, and consequently never received another chance? How many dropped catches could be related 'to the mind'?

Certainly, when relaxation is emphasized as an essential of performance, as is done by this book frequently, 'relaxation' does not mean total relaxation. No serious cricketer can be totally relaxed before or during a match, nor would we want him to be. What we mean, of course, is relaxed enough to get him out of over-stress into the zone of optimum stress. The zone of under-stress is seldom a danger.

It becomes obvious then that the *capacity to relax* is a vital attribute for the serious cricketer, whatever level he plays. In the long term, he must have other interests which will take him away from cricket both mentally and physically, whether these be family, friends, the garden, another career, reading, golf, the beach or

is destructive. To do so with players in the optimum stress zone is unnecessarily dangerous. Only with players in the under-stress zone does psyching-up make any sense at all. Yet such players are infrequent, we have found.

Over the years, I have seen so many young rugby or cricket teams subjected to the emotional pre-match psyche-up, then freeze up for the first fifteen minutes of a match. They found it difficult to pass, run or tackle, bat, bowl or catch, or think – all the things the coach has screamed at them. At last, after about fifteen minutes, they began to function as well as they

Fig 65   Each player must have his method of relaxation. Dennis Lillee finds one in the bath, with a paper and a joke. (Patrick Eagar)

fishing. But it must be something or somethings, and the coach/manager/parent can help the individual's long-term performance greatly by emphasizing and encouraging this search for other interests rather than a non-stop diet of cricket.

In the short term, before the match and during the match, each player must have his methods of relaxation. In the dressing room, this could be the old fashioned kip, reading, music, cards, yoga, humour, or team-mateship. It could mean getting out for a jog, a swim, a bat or bowl in the nets.

Such methods of relaxation are not only essential, they are individualistic.

It is unwise to be overly prescriptive about what form of relaxation is acceptable, just as it is unwise to insist on over-formalised warm-ups. Of ultimate importance must be what works for the individual, for in cricket the ability to relax is paramount. It is not only as a stress controller. In a game of unequalled demands on concentration, a balance of relaxation is essential. Most good concentrators are good relaxers, as I shall discuss in the next part on 'Concentration'.

A final comment: Many cricketers have fallen by the wayside, destroyed by their limited ability to relax. Ambition, determination, concentration, motivation are essential attributes to be a successful cricketer, but they demand a balance of relaxation to optimize performance.

Concentration

The most difficult part of batting, bowling, fielding or wicket-keeping is prolonged concentration. A slips fieldsman can come off the field after six hours without having taken one catch or fielded a ball, but still absolutely exhausted; because he has concentrated totally all day.

Non-cricketers cannot understand this. They denounce cricket as boring – 'watching the grass grow' – and not requiring fitness. They do not realize that a real cricketer is absorbed in everything that is going on around him – batting, bowling, wicket-keeping, fielding. And amidst that absorption, his concentration on his own particular job must be total. You cannot be bored whilst you are concentrating – that is a contradiction of terms – and to do so over long periods is exhausting at any level of fitness.

But it is a grossly misunderstood word itself, 'concentration'. So often the coach demands that the batsman should 'concentrate'. So often the captain exhorts his bowlers and fieldsmen to 'concentrate'. Yet seldom does anyone set out to explain clearly and simply what is meant by 'concentration'. Ask your batsman, ask your bowlers. What does 'concentration' mean? What do you do to 'concentrate' fully? Few will begin to give you a satisfactory answer, though the word has been hammered at them constantly. Let's try to answer the question.

BATTING

For a batsman, concentration is a twofold process. Firstly it means close focusing in on the ball, so that the eyes are aware of nothing else. *Nothing* else! I shall come back to 'close focus' later.

The other component of concentration is seldom mentioned. It is the simultaneous closed focus of the mind. By that, I mean that the mind must be cleared of all extraneous thoughts, of everything except staring at the ball, close focusing on it, one ball at a time. Thus I could be staring at the ball, close focusing, seeing nothing else at the point of delivery, but still have lost concentration. If the smallest part of my mind is thinking about anything else – wicket conditions, the quality of the bowler, what shot I should play, how well or badly I am batting, the presence of the selectors, my score, the weather etc., etc. – I have lost concentration. How often does a batsman get out when he begins to think it is his day and there is a hundred there for the taking? He has lost concentration, regardless of what his eyes are doing.

And the process must be *one ball at a time*. Only the one about to arrive matters. To think of the last ball once the bowler begins his approach, or the next, even momentarily, is a loss of concentration. To allow yourself to become angry or emotional is a certain way to lose concentration.

BOWLING

When you steady yourself before each delivery, you finalize your thoughts about what you intend to bowl this ball and where you wish to bowl it. Let's imagine you have decided to bowl a wrong'un, a bit quicker, well up, just outside off-stump.

Having made that decision, you begin your run-up rhythmically, preparing to enter into your delivery and spin the ball hard. Your eyes are staring at your target (whatever it may be – this we shall discuss later) *and* you clear your mind of everything else except what you want to bowl and where you are bowling it. You cannot be thinking of how much the ball is turning, who the batsman is, how many wickets you have – all of those are a loss of concentration. All you can do each ball to maximize your chance

of a wicket is to bowl what you want to bowl *this ball* and where you want to bowl it. So that is all your mind should concentrate on. Ball by ball. One at a time. You are not bowling ten overs; you are bowling sixty balls, one after the other.

Of course that does not mean that you have no overall plan; each ball may well be helping the next in achieving that plan. But the fact remains that to achieve the plan your first task is to bowl what you want where you want it, ball by ball. Without that discipline, any plan is meaningless. Nor does it mean that by such total concentration – two-fold concen-

Fig 66 Abdul Qadir steadies himself. He finalizes his thoughts for his next ball, and begins to stare at his target. (Patrick Eagar)

Fig 67 Peter Sleep moves into his delivery with eyes concentrating on his target, *not* on his footmarks. (Patrick Eagar)

tration – all errors will disappear. There are other ways you can get out apart from loss of concentration; other ways you can bowl a bad ball apart from concentration. But the majority of errors do come from inadequate concentration, and if you can minimize, or eventually, eliminate loss of concentration as a cause of mistakes, your performance will improve enormously and rapidly.

You must practise your concentration. That should be a major part of any practice. When experiencing poor practice conditions, you can always practise concentration when you cannot do much else. And never, never, never should you accept half-concentration – indeed anything less than total concentration – in any practice situation. It is a skill to master, the most important skill of all.

Remember this. Most losses of concentration come because we expect ourselves to lose concentration at some stage, and condone this in ourselves. Others come because we do not know how to concentrate.

Well, I have given you some ideas on *how* to concentrate now. I can also tell you that there is no logical reason why you should *ever* lose concentration. Just as no individual has ever fully utilized that wonderful brain he has been given, so no individual has ever fully utilized his capacity to concentrate. Even Sir Donald Bradman! There is no reason why you cannot concentrate forever if you believe you can. There is no reason why you should lose concentration unless you believe you will. With one proviso! Do not expect to concentrate all day, batting, bowling or fielding, without any

break. What we have to do is to learn to switch concentration on and off, and the ally of concentration is always relaxation.

As we steady ourselves before delivery, we begin to concentrate fully (as described), doing so during approach, delivery, follow through and the play that follows. Then when the ball is dead, we relax partially, and walk back whilst reviewing the last ball, the overall plan and the next ball. Back to the mark, steady yourself, make your decision on the next ball, then concentrate totally. At the end of the over, we relax and think whilst moving to our fielding position, where we turn our concentration powers on totally to our fielding duties. But, between each ball again we switch to a brief semi-relaxation. At drinks, lunch, tea and between wickets – any break in play – the relaxation should be more total.

Most sport demands high degrees of concentration, and usually, the higher the level, the greater the demands. But the nature of cricket probably increases the demands. Sustained concentration is an essential requisite for a successful cricketer, and to sustain it a complementary prerequisite is the ability to relax and to switch rapidly from concentration to relaxation and back. You will need to develop both skills to succeed as a wrist-spinner. Practise them like any other skills.

A FEW POST-SCRIPTS!

Previously I mentioned *close focus* and I would like to expand on that. A major part of being a skilled 'ball-game player' is 'ball sense', and part of that at least is automatic close focus. It is something you do not need to explain to, or drill, those who have developed it naturally in their child-hood, usually before eight years of age – those who spent most of their hours playing with some type of ball in those early years. But there is an increasing number today who have not had such an upbringing, they do not automatically close focus, and they need to be taught and drilled. Some of them are higher up in the game than you might expect.

Let me explain from the batting point of view first. When a coach asks a batsman 'Are you watching the ball?' he deserves that batsman's sharp rejoinder, 'Of course I bloody am!' Of course, he *is* watching the ball. But he may not be close *focusing* on it.

Try this exercise using Fig 68. Where you are sitting near the nets, look up to the far end of the ground. You will see the school buildings, the trees behind, the ground in front. You see the balcony, the clock tower above it, with the flag fluttering above it in the breeze. Now look at the clock tower only. If you stare at it, other details already mentioned fade into a haze. Now focus on the clock itself. Then to the hands of the clock. And finally onto the *junction* of the hands of the clock. That spot only! If you are concentrating hard on that one spot, close focusing in on it, everything else fades away, you can hardly see any-thing else at all.

That is how a natural ball player watches the ball. He does not see the full picture. As the bowler runs in he cannot see him, or the sight screen,

or anything else. He can only see the ball. If he does become aware of any-thing else, he has lost close focus; has lost concentration. Many cricketers do not do that naturally. They do see the full picture 'with the ball in it', and are therefore not concentrating totally. They need to learn how to close focus.

How does this concern the wrist-spinner? Well it comes down to *tar-gets*. Remember I wrote, 'Your eyes are staring at your target (whatever it may be)'? Let's think about that.

Many believe that the bowler should close focus in on his target as he moves in to bowl. I'm not so sure of that, but you should try it. Certainly when you are bowling well, you really cannot see the batsman, and certainly batsmen do make preliminary move-ments, such as charging, to try to make the bowler look at the batsman and so break his concentration.

Many bowlers have used many dif-ferent targets successfully, so you should experiment with each to find what suits you best. The logical target is the spot on the ground where you want the ball to land. Just as you stare at that spot on the dart board where you want the dart to land, so, it would seem, you should stare at the spot on the pitch where you want the ball to land. That makes sense!

Don't try to bowl at a coin or similar small spot. That is asking too much, and it does not make sense to set unat-tainable goals. Give yourself a reason-able spot on the length and line you wish and, in a match, that spot will have to be created and seen only in your mind's eye.

Other bowlers have drawn imagin-ary lines, say from off and middle

Fig 68   Go through your close focus exercises with these buildings of the
Rossall School.

stumps and set out to bowl, well up, within those lines. Personally that suited me best. But others have used the stumps as a target. That does not make sense, when you use the dart analogy. But Dennis Lillee used that target, and it seemed to work for him. Others admit that they were not really aware of what they watched, but it seemed to work. Others simply bowled to the wicket-keeper.

Most, when questioned, felt that they could not really see the batsman when they were bowling well, so one quite popular target – of watching the batsman's feet – seems inappropriate.

My point is that many bowlers have used many different targets, and used them successfully. I have been in cricket too long to be over-prescriptive. I respect individual differences too much for that.

My personal conclusion is that the staring at a target is more significant than the target itself. For the act of staring keeps the eyes steady, which keep the head steady, which helps keep the shoulders steady. When a bowler is concentrating totally, whatever his target, these factors are common. When he begins to lose concentration, the head and shoulders become unsteady – perhaps because the eyes have strayed from their target.

There is a lot for you to think about and work on there. I shall leave you with a final very useful aid, the idea of which I first received from Bob Massie, the West Australian and Australian swing bowler. I'll call it the 'Circle of Concentration'. Draw a circle and inside it write down all the things over which you have control when you are bowling. These are the only things you should think about.

Now start writing down all the other things which a bowler often thinks about as he is bowling. Put them inside the circle if he has control over them, outside if he has no control. You should come out with a circle something like Fig 69.

BOWLER'S CIRCLE OF CONCENTRATION

Many players I have coached, understand me when I say, 'You were thinking outside the circle'. They will tell me, 'I let myself get outside the

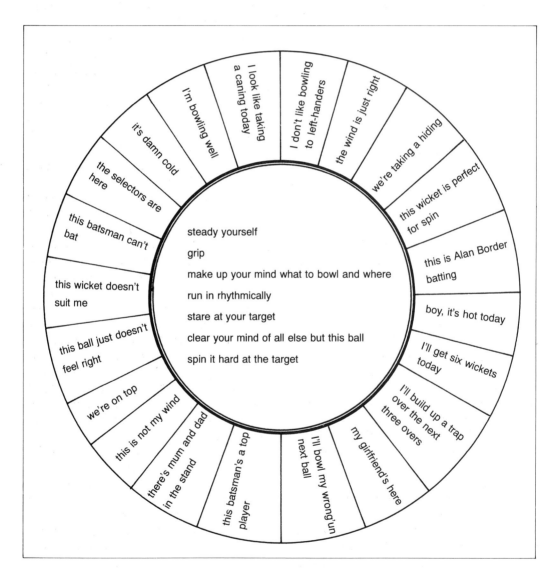

Fig 69   Think within the centre of the circle, not outside it.

circle'. It's a worthwhile concept. It emphasizes once again that the core of successful concentration is to hone in on those things over which you have control, and eliminate from your thinking anything over which you do not have control. Not a bad message for wrist-spinners – or, once again, for life as a whole!

Confidence

Most people are *not* over-confident or even very confident. Most of us have doubts and insecurities and usually it takes time and evidence to reassure us of our worth and comparative ability. Much of what I have written in this section on 'The Mind', relating to such matters as 'Motivation', 'Preparation', 'Stress Management', 'Relaxation', 'Concentration', relates to the establishment of self-confidence, as does the section on 'Attitude' in Chapter 4. But self-confidence is so basic, so vital, to maximum performance, that I shall sum it up again.

Many people adopt various ways of establishing and building their self-confidence. The variety is enormous and many psychologists live off it. Cricketers have resorted to motivational tapes, deep relaxation therapy, hypnosis – many cricketers, often, with successful results. Whatever helps you, as an individual, to promote your self-belief and self-esteem is worth while.

I have sometimes come across the player who truly believes that all his opponents are inferior – the batsman who 'knows' that he is better than any bowler; the bowler who has no doubt that he is superior to any batsman. To have such certain belief must be an enormous advantage for that player, though somewhat boring at times for his companions. If the belief is sincere, that player has no need to worry about what I have to say abut self-confidence.

Most of us are not like that person above. If as Curtly Ambrose runs in to bowl at me, I keep repeating 'You cannot bowl. You cannot bowl. I can bat better than you can bowl. I am superior etc., etc.', it does nothing for me as an individual. For another little voice inside my head begins to be heard saying 'That's not true, Pete. In fact he has more ability than you. He can bowl better than you can bat, BUT . . .' And though I am not one for 'buts' as you know, this 'but' is very important. Because I know I have a certain amount of ability, I have succeeded at school, at club level, at State level to Test level (or whatever level is relevant) and 'I have done it'. There is a reassuring basis of performance behind me. I know I have good levels of natural ability. In addition, I have worked hard over the years at practice, have accumulated knowledge, technique, experience. Another security platform. I have worked hard this season, performed well, am well prepared. More reassurance.

Further more I firmly believe in the concept of performance over result. My ambition is always to play as well as I possibly can, to give one hundred per cent, and receive the results I deserve. The bowler is a force beyond my control, so I do not spend too much time thinking of him, only of the ball in his hand. I shall concentrate

Fig 70   The awesome might of Curtly Ambrose in full flight. I would have to listen to the little voice inside my head. (Patrick Eagar)

totally on my performance, and it *will be* as good as I can make it. It will be one hundred per cent plus.

And cricket is a 'funny' game. If cricket were boxing, and Curtly and I met in the ring, alone, one to one, he would murder me. But this is not boxing, it is cricket. I have a team with me, we shall do it all together, and in this game the good team can defeat the better individuals – as long as each one of us and the team as a whole gives a hundred per cent.

I know I am well prepared, I know I have ability, there is no doubt I shall give everything I have, and certainly I would rather be out here than anywhere else. Because I love this silly bloody game. So I'll fight my heart

out, get stuck into this job and enjoy doing it. I don't give a stuff who the bowler is.

Now don't get me wrong! I am not going through this as Curtly runs in to bowl. I am not psyching myself up. It is something I know, deep inside, and it does not need some rhythmic, hypnotic chanting. Nor can such thoughts be false – a form of desperate rationalization. It is simply something that has developed with time within me, as much part of my cricket as my wrong'un and top-spinner.

And the same is true when I bowl. I do not really care who my opponent is. Of course, I shall have thought about him to construct a plan of attack if I feel it is necessary. Otherwise the answer must be to get on with it and do my thing, don't worry too much about him. *I'll bowl my very best and enjoy it, I have my fieldsmen there to support me, and when I bowl as well as I can, I have a good chance against anyone. All I need to worry about is simply doing my very best. So get on with it.*

What I have just outlined is the road to self-confidence that helped me. It was a road built on the sound foundations of self-knowledge, experience, and personal beliefs, not on the sands of artificial mumbo-jumbo or self-delusion. Over the years I have found that it has rung several bells with many cricketers. I hope it is of value to you.

The Enjoyment Cycle

This, too, is so vital that I must repeat it in this section. If you honestly enjoy what you are doing, you will relax

('relax' as I have discussed in the section above on 'Stress Management'). When you relax, you allow what you have to offer to come out unimpeded. When this happens, you are more likely to perform to the optimum. When you perform, you are more likely to achieve results. Performance (and results) give satisfaction, and satisfaction enhances enjoyment. And so on.

The cycle is self-perpetuating, but as I have said before, if you break it somewhere, you are in trouble. It needs rapid repair. If you try to begin the cycle without the initial premise, however, you simply have nowhere to go. This is a particular problem for full-time professional cricketers.

Don't Try too Hard

Just as 'relax' and 'concentrate' can be easily misunderstood, so can this one, 'Don't try too hard'. When you

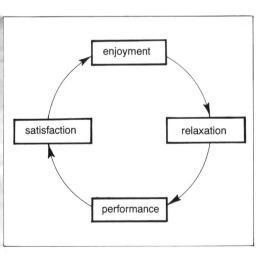

Fig 71 If you enjoy what you are doing, you will relax.

are constantly encouraged to do your very best, to always give a hundred per cent, it is very easy to try too hard, particularly when you are young and inexperienced, or when you are just clambering up onto a new rung of your personal ladder. 'Trying too hard' has certainly damaged a cricketer's performance far more often than 'not trying too hard'.

The answer to this problem has already been spelt out in the sections on 'Stress', 'Preparation', 'Performance vs Result', 'Enjoyment' and 'Confidence'. It is that, even though you stretch yourself and demand maximum effort, you must relax and let it happen. *Don't push too hard, don't strain.*

For the batsman, don't hit too hard or too early. Rely on your timing and patience. For the bowler, don't strain. Rely on your rhythm. Try to be confident, try to relax, try to enjoy it, try to let what you have got come out. It sounds easy, but it isn't! But it is so important. 'Don't try too hard'!

Perspective

It is always worth while remembering that you are a very small part of a great institution. Cricket has been doddering away for ages now; millions have played it, watched it, loved it, millions still do. The game itself is bigger than your national team, bigger than your provincial or club team, far bigger than you. Try not to do anything that will humiliate, embarrass or degrade this great old game. You are very fortunate to be part of it, and no matter who you are, you are after all only a humble part.

Yet cricket itself is only a very small and insignificant part of life and humanity. There are far more important things than cricket around us; the world would carry on without 'the flannelled fools'. There is 'life after cricket'.

It never does any player any harm to consider those thoughts occasionally. It helps to retain a balance, to keep a perspective, that helps make us better people, better cricketers. And that makes cricket a better game.

CHAPTER 6

Some Bowling Problems

PACE

Nothing is more likely to confuse and worry a young wrist-spinner more than the frequent advice he will receive on what pace he should bowl. The advice will come from all directions, often from those who should know better, and will frequently be contradictory. I can remember an old player telling me as I left the field, 'Throw them up, Peter. Slow down – You are bowling too fast.' Two minutes later inside the dressing room, the Captain asked me to push them through, 'Speed it up and get him back on the back foot'. It can be very confusing and very depressing, particularly when you are a teenager, you are growing, and the problem of changing trajectories is difficult enough anyway. For what it is worth, here is my advice on this subject.

There are different types of leg-spinners, who have individual advantages and disadvantages. The quicker leggie is usually a bigger, taller man, whilst the slower leggie is usually a shorter version. As I have said, they have differences but neither is necessarily right or wrong.

Unless he is like an O'Reilly, who was unique, the aims are similar. They are to confuse the batsman's judgement of length. The turn of the ball is

Fig 72 Not a big man, but a very quick leg-spinner and a fine one. B.S. Chandresekhar explodes through the crease and the ball is already on the way down. (Patrick Eagar)

not the only, or even, the major object. Turn, in fact, is only finishing off the confusion of length judgement which has resulted from subtle variations in trajectory and pace, drop, drift and bounce, which are created by vari-

Fig 73 Bob Holland, like most smaller men, was a slower leggie. See the ball going up, but Bob is still watching his target.

and decreases the deception of flight he depends upon. As a general rule, the ball should travel from the bowler's hand above eye level until it begins to drop. 'Never let batsman see top of ball', was the advice from an old Lancastrian spinner.

The answer is to bowl normally, and what comes out as you bowl normally is your pace. Of course, you may bowl faster on occasions for some tactical reason, and, of course, changing your pace will always be part of your attack. But your bread and butter pace, what you bowl ninety per cent of the time, is the one that is natural and comfortable. You should not strain beyond this, or you are likely to drop short. Nor should you slow down below this, or you will tend to lose 'oomph' and real spin, and become a lobber.

Remember what I suggested in Stage Three of the 'Eight Stages of Spin'. If you are running in, obtaining optimum momentum at delivery, bowling with both arms and your entire body, as well as the other spinning levers, exploding through the crease, half grunting to put zip on the ball, pivoting around the front leg, so that your bowling shoulder faces the batsman now, and finishing with a powerful follow through – if all those things are happening, then what comes out is your natural pace. Whether it be slower or quicker is immaterial; that is *your pace* and that is the speed you should bowl.

A warning! Read what I have said above carefully. If you are dawdling in, rolling the ball up, without oomph or body drive, using only one arm and simply lobbing them up, you are not

ations of over-spin, side-spin and back-spin. The side-spin which creates turn off the pitch is the best known and most easily recognized but, in fact, over-spin and back-spin are probably more significant ingredients of the leg-spinner's tactics.

Thus bowling faster in order to achieve quicker turn is seldom an advantage. It may be for an O'Reilly type, but for the normal spinner, a slow spinner, increased pace simply flattens the trajectory of the delivery getting the best out of yourself. At that stage you have not yet established your natural pace. Once you have established that, however, the question of what pace you should bowl should be wiped from your thinking. You should not be worrying about that again, for you have enough to do just getting on with your chosen form of bowling. If you are worrying about your pace, it is a certain way to break your concentration.

In future, just thank those who offer advice on pace politely. Then forget it, and bowl at what you know is your natural pace.

LINE

There will be times when you attack different lines – sometimes outside leg, other times at leg-stump, middle and off, even outside off-stump. Also, you will often change your line during an over tactically, for instance, widening outside off-stump. But amidst these changes, you will tend to have a bread and butter line, the normal line upon which you base your normal attack. There are arguments for different basic lines of attack.

1. Throughout cricket history, most wrist-spinners have bowled along *middle and off line to* right-hand batsmen and well outside off-stump to left-handers.

Let's take the right-hand batsman first.

If I keep at him along the middle and off line varying my spin, over the top, round the side, underneath, I have certain advantages.

(a) I can bring in my wrong'uns, top-spinners and back-spinners without the warning of a changed line.

(b) If I beat the bat on this line there is little chance of legs getting in the way to thwart stumpings and catches.

(c) On such a line, I can bowl to a strong off-side field. If I maintain line and length the batsman may be tempted to hit across my spin towards the leg side to penetrate the field. I should be happy for him to try that. Also, even if I drop short, the turn takes the ball towards the off where the fielding strength is.

(d) Bowling along that line, turning away, gives me the advantage of leaving the batsman's body and eyes. This gives me the same advantage as the outswing bowler who bowls along the famous 'line of uncertainty'.

2. *Outside off-stump to a packed off-field.* This seldom works even as the negative containment it aims at. For as soon as a leg-spinner bowls outside off-stump, point is opened up, and most quality batsmen are murder there. You end up needing three points – backward, square and forward – and you run out of fieldsmen.

Also, such a line with such a field is primarily negative and defensive. You are setting out to 'bore the batsman out' and that is not the mental approach we would like to see wrist-spinners take too often.

3. *Leg-stump line* makes a lot of sense. It creates the same effect as the off-spinner bowling outside off-stump, in that it forces the batsman to play against the spin. But it has several disadvantages. Your wrong'uns, top-spinners and back-spinners are less effective on this line, and you must have pin-point accuracy. For the fuller ball will be hit on the on-side, and the short ball, with the turn, on the off-side. It is difficult to defend both sides of the wicket at once. Furthermore the batsman's body and legs get in the way. Potential stumpings and catches behind, forced by drop, drift, bounce and turn are thus frustrated.

4. *Wide of leg-stump* – often from round the wicket. This is usually to take advantage of foot-marks, and it can be over-done. The point is that it should signal to a reasonably intelligent batsman that you are trying to bowl him around his legs. At that stage, he can take block outside leg-stump, always cover your turn with his body and legs, and wait.

I feel that the wrist-spinner who has control of the large leg-break can best utilize those foot marks by bowling over the wicket along middle and off line, camouflaging his plan, then throwing in the big leg-break wide of leg-stump, full, into the footmarks, and inviting a poorly executed sweep shot.

Furthermore, this form of bowling – round the wicket, wide of leg-stump – as practised in England these days, can simply become another form of negativism.

To the left-hand batsman.
Most left-hand batsmen are strong on their legs. They will deal violently with the leg-spinner who strays into their legs by bowling too much at the stumps.

The leg-spinner must attack him wide of off-stump where there are usually some foot marks. If he keeps the ball up along that line, little can go wrong. In fact, it is better to start too wide then work in to the correct line, than start too close to the stumps, then try and work out. Most left-hand batsmen do not like to be forced to play across wide on the off to deliveries which are likely to drop and spin back sharply into them. This is further complicated by the occasional wrong'un leaving him, and top-spinners and back-spinners going on. All these varieties should be bowled along that same line – wide of off-stump and well up.

As I have said you will vary your line at times as part of your tactics, but you do need to establish a normal basic line of attack that suits you best. Only then can you finalize your basic field setting.

FIELD PLACEMENT

Remember that with the variety he has available and if he spins the ball hard, the leg-spinner can never be negative. By the very nature of his bowling, he is an aggressive, positive bowler. Thus he does not need ultra-attacking fields to justify his credentials.

A leg-spinner may like to start with two on the boundary at square-leg and mid-wicket. If it makes him comfortable as he sets out to spin the ball hard and throw the ball up, let him have them. After all, quicks often bowl with a fine-leg and third-man without being accused of negativism. As the leggie settles down, he may choose to bring in one or both boundary riders, but, if he is more comfortable with them out there, give them to him.

Very seldom does a leg-spinner benefit from a bat-pad fieldsman. There may be occasions when he may wish to crowd the bat, but generally he does not like or use such close fieldsmen. The modern argument is that bat-pads put pressure on batsmen, but more often than not they put more pressure on the bowler, who in response, tends to tighten up, reduce variation, speed up, and flatten in order to bowl to that field.

On good wickets good batsmen thrive on bat-pad fieldsmen. Two such fieldsmen remove two from the in-field, gaps open up, runs are more easily come by, and pressure reduces. A far more worrying fieldsman to the batsman in full cry on a good wicket is short cover, short mid-on or short mid-wicket about twenty yards from the bat. So don't forever force close fieldsmen on leg-spinners. For some, never use them, for others, use them as a variation, for none make them a permanent tactic. Remember that a leg-spinner is often more effective if you withdraw the field, loosen the batsman up and encourage him to play shots, rather than trying to tighten him up with close-set fields.

A captain should always think of his nine fielders as pawns to be used as each situation demands. It is limiting to become too rigid in your planning of set, pre-conceived field placements. Of course there are basic bread and butter fields, but always be prepared to improvise. I recommend the old captaincy adage: 'If you think of something which is a positive, aggressive change, don't wait, do it at once. If you think of a change which is negative and defensive, don't hurry into it, it can wait.'

For a basis of discussion, I set out below traditional, orthodox field placements for a right-hand leg-spinner to a right-hand batsman and a left-hand batsman. Following these are a few explanatory notes.

1. **To a right-hand batsman** in normal circumstances, that is, on a good wicket, attacking middle and off-stump.

(a) Slip must be positioned carefully according to the type of leg-spinner. The slower, bigger turner may require a wider, closer slip whilst the quicker leggie may have him deeper and straighter. But based on your experience you must place him exactly where you want him and not simply settle for 'a slip'.

(b) Short extra cover is a major attacking fieldsman for a leg-spinner. Not too close, about fifteen to twenty yards from the bat he is far enough back to see and catch anything hit at him. The slightly lofted drive is out, a worrying thought for any batsman if the ball is drifting, dropping, bouncing and turning.

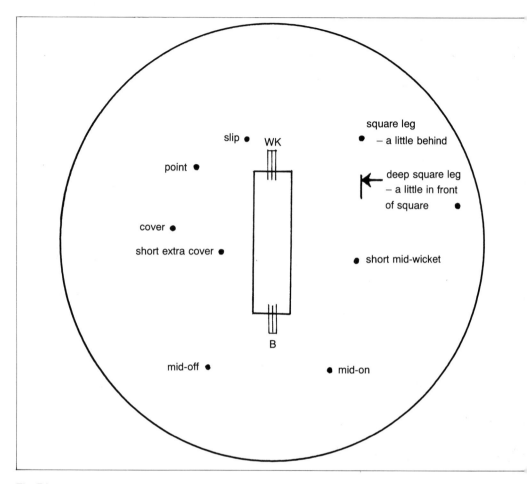

Fig 74.

(c) With the short extra-cover, mid-off and cover can be a little deeper yet still stop the single, particularly if the bowler and short-cover move quickly towards the ball and so hold the striker back momentarily. Remember *in-fieldsmen must stop singles*; a failure to do so makes it very difficult to bowl as batsmen constantly change ends.

(d) Mid-wicket too can be useful shortish for the same reasons as extra-cover, particularly if the bowler values his wrong'un.

(e) Few leg-spinners have ever bowled without one on the boundary; many used two particularly in opening overs. Perhaps when the leg-spinner has settled down the out-fieldsmen may be brought in to strengthen the in-field or close-catchers.

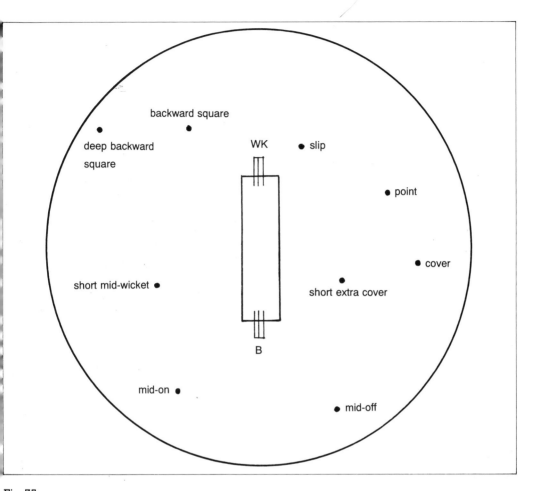

Fig 75.

(f)   Note that only two fieldsmen plus the keeper are behind the wicket and the straight-hit field is very strong. If I am trying to spin the ball hard, getting it to drop, drift and turn, keeping it well up, and encouraging batsmen to drive, this is the way the field should be. On occasions, I watch leg-spinners bowl with a backward-point, slip, short-backward square, deep-back- ward square and keeper, all behind the wicket. What can their plan be when half the team is fielding behind the stumps?

2. **To a left-hand batsman** in normal circumstances, on a good wicket, trying to bowl well up about a foot outside the left-hander's off-stump where there are usually some scuff marks.

(a) Much the same as the right-hander's field, in reverse. The bowler must aim to keep well outside off-stump. If his line begins to squeeze into the left-hander's legs, he will be worked away easily on the on-side or even carved up.

(b) To the left-hander both square-legs, short and deep, should be behind square, because of the direction of turn.

(c) For the same reason, short mid-wicket becomes as significant as short-cover was for the right-hander.

(d) Slip is probably finer now.

(e) Short-cover is still important, particularly if the bowler values his wrong'un.

(f) Same comments as for out-fieldsmen and in-fieldsmen.

What I have outlined above are basic, orthodox field placements adopted by orthodox leg-spinners over the last fifty years. They are worthy of your consideration.

WINDS

The wind always interested me far more than the wicket. There are few wickets that you will not be able to turn enough on, if you give it a flick. And, if you have the right breeze, it will increase drop, drift, bounce and turn.

The wrist-spinner should wish to bowl against ninety-nine per cent of winds. Coming from over third-man, it will aid drop and bounce, in-drift for your leg-spinner, and turn for your wrong'un. Straight on, it helps everything. From over fine-leg the wrong'un drifts, the leg-break drops and turns. You should be happy with all of those.

Cross breezes can be annoying, but when they occur, you should use them for their drift. That means you bowl from the end where the breeze is coming across from the off-side.

Perhaps you may come across a slow turner where you decide to bowl downwind. But I would still be doubtful. Perhaps you may find a gale where you decide to come down-wind. But again I would be doubtful. For to desert the advantage of bowling into the wind, is to ignore everything this book has outlined. Turn, for most of us, only finishes off what has happened in the air – the drift, drop, the flight which must be accentuated by a head wind. When the breeze is up your tail, you lose all of that, the ball is carried on, and you become totally dependent on turn. You are less likely to confuse a batsman's judgement of length.

The worst possible reason I have heard for bowling with the wind is so that the batsman must hit into it when lofting. What negative thinking. If any batsman wants to try and slog you, take him on with your drop, drift and turn. Turn it big, vary your flight, and bowling into the wind will help you. Don't be frightened of big hitters. The spinning, flighted ball is harder to hit safely than balls from medium-pacers are.

Fluky, changeable breezes can be annoying. You go on one end and it seems to change. You go on the other end and it seems to change again. The

Fig 76 Jim Higgs spins the ball hard up into the breeze. Higgs was one of
Australia's best leg-spinners since the war.

danger becomes that you are worrying more about wind direction than bowling. You begin to think of matters over which you have no control and hence lose concentration. On such occasions, make a decision, then stick to it. Forget the wind and get on with your job. Better to be bowling at the wrong end than not at all.

There is another practical reason to want and learn to bowl into the wind. The quicks will want to bowl with it, and there is no more penetrative attack than the real quick down-wind and the real spinner up-wind.

Stronger-than-usual winds often worry many wrist-spinners or swing-bowlers. They tend to fight it. They feel they have to bowl a little faster to counter-act the effect of the breeze. Thus they push themselves and over-strain. The answer is never to fight a strong head wind. On the contrary, go with it, use it, play with it. Nowhere is that better illustrated than at Perth, when the afternoon Fremantle Doctor steams in fresh and strong. Experienced Western Australian swing bowlers glory in bowling against it, throwing the ball up, bending it all over the place, never fighting it. The same applies to experienced spinners in Perth. It is a beautiful place to bowl wrist-spinners. It will bounce and turn, and if you go along with the breeze sensibly, the ball will drift and drop all over the place.

Sydney and Perth were my favourite first-class grounds to bowl on, because of the breeze. The West Indian grounds had the same advantage. There were always fresh sea breezes on the islands. That my best results were on these grounds, bowling into the available wind, was no coincidence.

So when you wake up on the morning of the game, check the wind. When you get to the ground, before you check the wicket, check the wind. Which end is best for you? After a lifetime of this, it is still automatic for me, and I look with dismay at those people, who, after the start of play are heard to say, 'Which direction is the wind coming from?' As a wrist-spinner, don't ever allow your ignorance to show like that.

WICKETS

We all spend our lives inspecting wickets and trying to predict how they will play, and we all keep making mistakes. With experience we should get better, but I've met no-one who reads them all to perfection. So the best thing as a wrist-spinner is not to worry too much about them. Be more interested in the breeze!

Wrist-spinners ('who give them a flick') want to bowl on hard, firm wickets. Wickets that will bounce, come onto the bat, and only offer turn to those who really spin the ball. Wrist-spinning was developed for bowling on such wickets. They don't really want the dusty 'square turner', or the 'damp popper', or 'the sticky'. These are the wickets that finger-spinners and sometimes seamers can thrive on. But of course, if we get a chance to bowl on these we do so willingly.

On the slower wickets, there is the temptation and often the encouragement 'to push the ball through', to bowl faster. For most wrist-spinners, unless you are naturally the quicker type, that can be a mistake. On a slow turner, you want the batsman to drive. As the ball turns square and holds up, driving can be hazardous in such conditions. Thus the ball must be kept well up.

For most wristies the most certain method of keeping the ball up, is to bowl a little slower. Straining and bowling above normal pace often leads to dropping short, and regardless of its pace, batsmen murder short deliveries on such wickets. So, if anything, I tended to bowl slower on slow turners, kept it well up and spun it square. Then the batsman had 'to do all the hitting'. You should try that out, and see if it suits you.

Another common danger for the spinner is caused by the 'crumbling, turning wicket'. Now everyone says, 'It's your day here. You'll get a bag'. So out you go, try to bowl everything, try to bowl everyone out, and disappoint yourself. The answer must be to bowl normally, be patient, and don't try too hard. Just run up, bowl well and the wickets will come.

Dampish, skidding wickets can create a problem. The ball becomes hard to grip and with your normal wrist-spinners the turn goes. In my later years, however, as long as I could still hold the ball, I found the back-spinner very useful in such conditions. It skidded on, but went the opposite way to normal off the pitch. I don't know why, but it did. A bit of leg-spin amongst the back-spin and it ripped back from the off, then an orthodox off-spinner which went from the leg. Try it. If it works, keep a straight face and let them believe you have bowled the unpickable wrong'un.

OTHER PROBLEMS

Teenage Trajectory

Many a young wrist-spinner has seen a promising career delayed or finished around the early to mid-teens. Almost without exception, it has been after one of those gigantic teenage growth spurts.

For years, the little boy had looped up his leg-spinners and wrong'uns, turning and flighting the ball with great success. Now this gangling youth, far taller than the little boy inside him, seems to have lost all his accuracy, loop, confidence – the lot. The problem is that his eyes are now seeing the pitch and the batsman from new angles, and from the newly achieved height the old tried and trusted trajectory is no longer working. It can be a very frustrating and traumatic stage, and some boys have even turned away from the

heaven of wrist-spin to the hell of sea-mers because of it.

The cure is patient, sympathetic encouragement. The teenager *will* change his trajectory, but he *must not set out to do so*. The answer is for him to go on doing the normal things – all the levers, both arms and the body etc., etc. – and the adjustments will come. He must not set out to actively alter his pace, trajectory etc. but just let it happen. And as it does, gradually, we are there to reassure and encourage – certainly not to criticize, hassle, and suggest all the hopeless remedies he must try to cure this most natural problem of growing up.

The Lost Leg-Break

This is very common for the bowler who has just discovered his wrong'un. In his joy of new discovery, he over bowls the new toy and suddenly finds that his faithful old leg-break no longer functions.

Best to avoid this tragedy in the first place by never bowling too many consecutive wrong'uns as you learn it. Never more than about one in ten amongst the leg-breaks and top-spinners, as you learn. That way your mind remembers what the hand must do. But, if it is too late to be wise, and the leg-break has gone, the answer is to help the mind remember the hand's job. Begin under-arm bowling a series of leg-breaks and wrong'uns, watching carefully what your hand must do to perform these tasks. Now go to round arm. You can still see what is happening there, so watch carefully. Eventually when you feel you have given the confused mind an adequate refresher course, go back to over-arm. There it must function unseen and if your mind cannot quite cope with it yet, go back to under-arm and round-arm for a little more observation. Be patient. This will work for you if you give it time. It will be worth it, for you will have your leg-break back, and your new toy, the googly, will be still there too. Now, for goodness sake, be careful. Don't over-use the googly again and be forced to repeat this process.

Over and Round the Wicket

On most occasions you will bowl over the wicket. It is preferable to be in close to the stumps, so that you bowl along the line of the stumps. Also, when you learn to bowl close to the stumps it is easy to go wide as a variation, but get used to bowling wide out and it is usually very hard to get back in close.

There will be occasions to bowl round the wicket for tactical reasons. One of these should *not* be that you always bowl around the wicket to a left-hand batsman. Normally, to bowl round to a left-hander angles the ball in towards his legs, which is what he prefers.

Nevertheless you will bowl around the wicket on some occasions. Thus you must practise it. Make sure that you practise bowling around the wicket quite regularly, so that when you need to do so, it is quite comfortable and normal.

Bowling to Tail-Enders

As a wrist-spinner, you and the bowler of real pace are those most likely to dismiss tail-enders quickly. And 'wrapping up the tail' quickly is vital for teams who wish to win.

When you get your chance to bowl at the tail, do not try too hard and do not fall into the trap of expecting too much too quickly. Simply settle down and bowl patiently. If you bowl as well as you can, accurately, that will usually be enough. No need to go through your array of variations, which are likely to be wasted on the tail, and, which, if you are not careful, can create inaccuracy and reduce pressure.

If the tail-ender is right-handed, it is your bread and butter leg-break which leaves him and is most likely to cause him trouble. So bowl normally, vary your pace, be patient, and concentrate on one ball at a time. Do not begin to fire in wrong'uns, top-spinners, flippers etc. amidst a growing frustration of impatience.

Showing your Frustration

If getting angry with yourself or outwardly showing your frustration helped you to bowl more effectively, I would say 'go ahead!' But, for the majority of us, it doesn't. Nothing is more likely to break concentration than losing your cool. Nothing is more likely to give a batsman psychological dominance than watching the bowler kick the pitch, swear at himself or others, or in any other way outwardly display frustration.

You must *swallow that frustration*, force yourself to forget what has stirred you up, and get on to the next ball – the only one that ever matters. That does not mean you are always accepting and prepared to be walked over. Not at all! But aggression comes through more forcefully from actions and body language than from heated, undisciplined words. If in doubt, shut up!

The Problem of Advice

Every young cricketer, particularly if he is blessed with talent, is open to an enormous amount of advice during his career from a large variety of people. Many of these people know what they are talking about, many do not. Most are absolutely sincere in their desire to help you, some are not. Often the best advice can come from the most unlikely sources; often the most apparently qualified adviser offers poor advice *for you*.

Does that sound confusing? It should do, because it is, particularly when you are young and your career has just begun. Facing this dilemma, many young players decide to ignore all advice, and rely totally on themselves. This is a pity, for such players can ignore excellent advice which could save them much time – or even more. On the other hand, others take all advice as gospel, and try to fit it all into their game. This can lead to great confusion, frustration and disappointment.

As usual, the answer to the problem lies somewhere between these two extremes. The wise young player – indeed any player of any age – should listen to all advice, and thank the people who offer it politely. Then he must go away and consider that advice, and, within his experience, he must decide whether that advice is suitable for him as an individual or not. No-one else can make that decision. At some stage, every individual must face that fact. His own personal destiny does lie in his own hands and it is his responsibility. Not his captain's, his coach's, or his father's.

Never rely totally on the advice of others, but never ignore advice. Think, and work it all out. Of course, what you read here is someone's advice – this entire book is my advice. I certainly do not expect you to take any of it as gospel. Think over what you read. Does it make sense? Is it good advice? Does it suit you? In the long run only you can answer these final questions?

A final bit of advice on the subject – for your consideration. Over my lifetime, I have come to believe that most advice that is simple and logical – it makes sense – is usually the 'correct' advice. When it is complicated and obscure, beware! Think that over, too!

CHAPTER 7

Advanced Tactics

I have spent many hours sitting through pre-match dinners and conferences on the eve of first-class matches, usually analysing and discussing the weaknesses and strengths of opponents. Often what was said was positive and useful, but just as often it became negative and counter-productive.

It is very easy to become obsessive in this minute analysis of the opposition. The danger is that if you spend too much time thinking and worrying about *them*, you allow them to dominate your thinking, and you are likely to spend too little time concentrating on *your own role*. Generally speaking, if each individual does his own job as well as he can, and the team does its job as well as it can, the eventual performance will bring successful results.

That does not mean that you do not think carefully about your opponents. You do, you will discuss them and, on occasions, individual weaknesses and strengths will be identified and methods of exploiting and combating them planned. But keep this in perspective. You must not fall too easily into a pattern of bowling *dictated by your opponent's actions*. For, as much and as often as possible, you should force the batsman to bat against you, rather than you bowl against him. The two statements sound similar, but there is a huge mental difference when you think them over carefully.

You, as the bowler, wish to *dominate* and maintain the ascendancy. You wish to choose the ground and build the pressure. He is the one who should be doing the countering. If you are not careful, obsessive concern about him and his weaknesses and strengths can undermine that fundamental goal.

So you bowl and attack him, whoever he is. If your initial form of attack is less successful than you had hoped and he is gradually beginning to put more pressure on you than you on him, try something else. Don't stagnate. No need for excessive change, such as a sudden increase of variety, with all types of wrong'uns, top-spinners, flippers etc. being unleashed. That is panic, which usually leads to inaccuracy, rapidly decreased pressure and your defeat.

Small changes are enough. A change of line, from off-stump to leg-stump or vice versa. A change of field – bring it in or spread it out. A change of pace or angle. Or a change of your pattern of over-spin, side-spin and under-spin. Any of these will do. The purpose is to *force the batsman to start again*. He has begun to obtain dominance and confidence, so you do something different, force him to change his plan and pattern, and make him think again. That is all part of making him bat against you, rather than vice versa.

In first-class cricket (but seldom anywhere else) the time will come when you simply must defend and plug away. You bowl tight and wait. That will happen to us all. But don't allow it to happen too often or too easily. For many bowlers, that is their immediate response when they sense a loss of ascendancy. First they should explore other methods of attacking and maintaining dominance, before they give in to negativism.

For that is what containment is. It is openly revealing your acceptance of the batsman's upper hand, that you have given in and are now prepared to bowl to him rather than making him bat to you.

Having the experience and confidence to come up with tactical changes becomes vital in the longer game of first-class cricket where few batsmen are poor players.

Again I recall those analyses of opposition batsmen over many negative hours which concluded that ninety per cent of them had a particular weakness – the perfect length ball, on the line of off-stump, which left them late. Of course they did! We all do!

You will come across some batsmen in first-class cricket with a particular weakness or strength which can be worked on. Some examples are:

1.   The front-foot committer who wants to get at you and drive on the off-side, even to the extent of running around the ball in order to hit it on the off-side.

2.   The fluent top-hand player, who hits beautifully straight, particularly towards off, but finds any cross-bat shot less natural.

3.   The bottom-hand player who wants to cut and pull everything.

4.   The player who for one of several technical reasons, tends to hit across the ball regularly.

5.   The front-foot committer who wants to get down the track at you all the time.

6.   The back-foot committer who is loathe to ever leave his crease.

7.   The compulsive six-hitter.

8.   The player who is particularly worried about 'picking you'.

9.   The attacking batsman who is a confirmed strike stealer.

10.   The defensive batsman, who, though bogged down, still tries to dominate the strike.

Those are ten types to think about and I offer the following thoughts.

A plan for 1 has already been dealt with in Chapter 3. You should notice that there I suggest you play along with his strength before attacking the weakness, rather than immediately targeting in on the weakness alone. Think about that.

The same could apply to 2, though

I would probably choose to switch my attack permanently to leg-stump or just outside leg-stump to such a player, keeping the ball well up. This could force him into sweeping against his will, or tie him up, or lead to a caught-and-bowled as he drove unnaturally at this new line.

For 3, I must be full, even if it means slowing down, concentrating on the bread and butter leg-spin, and trying to force him to drive. As well, I would zoot in the occasional back-spinner at the line of the stumps.

With 4, we could try much the same plan, with the line more at off-stump, or just outside.

With 5, earlier in my career, I would have kept on spinning hard over the top, throwing the ball up and gradually widening on him. But as the years went by, I would have zooted back-spinners at him, holding him back and hoping to frustrate him and/or change his plan of attack, then thrown up the top-spinning leggie a little wider of off-stump.

For 6, we must not allow him what he wants, that is, to stay comfortable defending from the crease, then picking off anything short. We must be right up there, often throwing up the over-spinner, trying to drag him forward and out, against his will. If we can frustrate him, the flipper or back-spinner in line with stumps could force the final error to finish him.

For 7 my plan would be similar to that proposed against 5.

Type 8 is far more frequent than you might think at first-class level. Let him see the wrong'un early, perhaps even the back-spinner or flipper. Then hide them away and bowl away tightly, con-centrating on leg-spin and slight changes of pace, whilst he reads what he wants into it all.

Types 9 and 10 can be exploited by you and your captain working together to take valuable wickets. With 9, based on changing field placement and your accuracy, par-ticularly early and late in the over, restrict him and keep him away from the strike as much as possible. With 10, do the opposite; give him the strike as much as possible. If you can maintain such tactics, you are likely to see growing frustration, some division in the opposition camp, and some strange shots and running between the wickets.

I offer those ten examples cau-tiously. For it can be a mistake for bowlers to believe that there is some magical formula for the dismissal of each batsmen – that the experienced bowler can immediately categorize batsman number 1 as being such and such type, and just as immediately dispense plan A to destroy him. As each batsman comes in, he is similarly categorized, and the magic formulae produced.

It simply does not happen that way. As I have said, over the years, you will detect certain types of players and devise a method of attacking them. And you will remember certain indi-viduals and do the same. But, day in, day out, in first-class cricket, it is not as easy as that. These are quality play-ers, or they would not be there. They have ability and experience, and many of the better ones will have no obvious dent in their armour. Then you set about your tasks as I have described. Attack your chosen line, use your variations subtly, probe away and try to establish pressure. Try to make sure you are not mentally allowing yourself simply to bowl to him. Think, keep on thinking, and be prepared to innovate.

With most quality batsmen on quality wickets, you are not going to mesmerize them out. It will take time and patience, sensible variation, prolonged accuracy – eventually these can encourage a slight loss of concentration in the batsman and his self-defeat. Never is that more so than that awesome day when you come across your first wicket that does not turn at all. For most of us who give it a real flick that does not happen until first-class cricket, and even then not very often. But it will happen!

The answer then is not to panic, or try too hard. Do not spin any harder than we are accustomed to or rattle through all the variations. Nor should we give in and hope to be taken off defeated. We need to accept the situation as quickly as possible, shock though it may be, and continue to bowl naturally. We do not like the idea of not turning, but at the moment there is nothing we can do about it. So we choose line, relax, enjoy the contest, spin over-the-top for drop and bounce, round-the-side for drift and underneath for flatter trajectory and skid. We work away with what we have got – which is still quite a lot – forget what we could have, try to build pressure, maintain it, and stay cool.

Elsewhere in this book, I discuss some ideas about bowling wrist-spinners on wet wickets. That should be of interest to you. Look at the section on 'Wickets' in Chapter 6.

Fig 77 John Gleeson cleverly utilized the methods of Jack Iverson. This led to a change, late in his career, from an average wicket-keeper/batsman to a successful Test match spinner.

A final thought. Later in my career, when I had good control over my back-spinners, I began to work on them in much the same way as the over and side-spinners. Remember 'going around the loop' and the variation of angles of spin? What I began to try and do was to vary the amount of back-spin and, often in combination with the height of arm at delivery – round-arm to slightly past-the-vertical – to vary the direction of skid off the wicket. That is, you set out to make some balls skid away, some straight on and some back in. It was fascinating, and opened up another entire workshop of variation – still, of course, inter-mixed with side-spin and over-spin. Unfortunately, it was towards the end of my playing career and I did not have the years or the overs to pursue what was necessary. Perhaps you have!

Remember the rewards offered to the innovators of cricket over the years. Imagine the impact of the first men to swing the ball at will. What of the man who bowled the first googly? Or flipper? Look into the interesting innovations of Jack Iverson and John Gleeson, if you don't already understand them. Or find out about Sonny Rhamadhin. The point is that *there is always something new.* Someone will find it! If it is you, you will reap a rapid reward – as long as you do not get carried away and forget that all your variations, plans and tactics can only succeed if they are based on control and accuracy.

Think about those back-spinners. Get a ball and experiment. Spin away again, but, this time, 'around a *bigger loop*'!

CHAPTER 8

A Philosophy of Wrist-Spin Bowling and the Role of Captains, Selectors and Clubs

A PHILOSOPHY OF WRIST-SPIN BOWLING

As a young cricketer, I grew up in an age where wrist-spin was an integral part of cricket and had been since time immemorial. Players understood it and its role in the game. From the 1970s, however, changes in attitude, method and tactics came which proved disadvantageous to wrist-spin. Whether such changes prove to be permanent remains to be seen, but recent developments do point to a revival of interest in the wrist-spin art.

Two decades is a long time in cricket. In that time, players developed who had little contact with, hence understanding of, wrist-spin bowling. Many became captains. If wrist-spin is to return to the game at all levels – which it could well do – there are likely to be many who would benefit from a refresher course in the entire philosophy of wrist-spin bowling. That is what I have set out to do here in brief.

It could be argued that what follows is simply my philosophy. But, I believe, it is more than that. It is the philosophy towards wrist-spin that I grew up with during the 1940s, 1950s and 1960s which has been handed on by generations of Australian cricketers at least, who believed wholeheartedly in wrist-spin as an integral part of the game of cricket as they knew it. In those days every club team in Sydney fielded at least one or two wrist-spinners, most State sides fielded at least one (with New South Wales, arguably the home of wrist-spinners, often playing three or four) and an Australian side without a wrist-spinner was virtually unknown. That is the way it had always been in Australian cricket.

You will note the word 'aggressive' frequently used in the discussion which follows. It is meant here as attacking and positive, not as the boorish verbal abuse and threatening physical gesticulations which, these days, are referred to as 'sledging'.

So to a philosophy of wrist-spin!

1. Cricket should be an aggressive, positive game whenever possible for the benefit of both players and spectators. This is even more so in professional cricket, as professional cricketers are also entertainers who have a duty to the game and the spectators to create as entertaining a spectacle as they can within the bounds of hard, serious competition.

2. In positive, aggressive cricket, the aim is to score runs as quickly as possible and take wickets as quickly as possible, in order to create time to win.

3. In every game played, you go into the match trying to win. You only try to save a game when winning becomes absolutely impossible. Better to lose, trying to win, that never to have tried at all. The ultimate negativism is to begin negatively, trying to save each match, then trying to win when the opposition has made errors.

4. You cannot expect to win consistently unless you can bowl teams out.

5. Under Australian conditions, in particular, the most successful method of taking wickets quickly over the years has been a combination of real pace and real spin.

6. Wrist-spin is therefore an integral part of positive, attacking cricket on hard wickets.

7. Thus a wrist-spinner must be primarily an attacking bowler.

8. To fill that role, he must:
(a) spin the ball hard;
(b) try to get the ball past the bat;
(c) have excellent control. Good wrist-spinners are *not* inaccurate; they must expect to bowl enough in practice and matches to attain accuracy. If they expect to be accurate then they will be;
(d) have good variation;
(e) have a desire to be aggressive and innovative;

(f) understand his craft, have the ability to detect batting weaknesses, have the tactical knowledge and experience to cope with them.

9. There will be times when he must bowl tight and defend, but that should be the leg-spinner's last card. Normally if the game gets bogged down, he should try something different, be innovative in his desire to attack. He needs to have such alternatives amidst his tactics.

This one needs some expansion. Of course, every bowler meets the situation where he must simply knuckle down and bowl tight to try and maintain pressure. It is possible that he may even be forced to fall into the role of trying to 'bore the batsman out'.

Many bowlers reach that stage too quickly, however. It becomes an automatic second nature, without really thinking of anything else.

The true wrist-spinner should try to dictate the game to the batsman whilst he can. Of course he must have accuracy but he should have the variations to attack. He may go around the wicket, change his line, change his plan, change his field – anything rather than allow the game to become stagnant. He should try to 'make the play', force the batsman to 'bat against him'. Maintain the ascendancy before giving into a plugging role of containment too easily. For whoever dictates the play and creates the most pressure, usually wins the game.

10. Motto – 'If you think of something aggressive and positive, do it at once.

If you think of something negative and defensive, don't hurry into it, think it over, it can wait.'

11. To do all of the above, the wrist-spinner must bowl a great deal in practice of all types and matches. He must want to bowl under all circumstances and be confident the ball will go where he wants it to go as he spins it hard.

12. Develop the philosophy that he is more interested in bowling well than in results. If he continues to bowl well, perform well, then results must come. He has control over his performance, but no control over results. Never waste time worrying about things over which you have no control. 0 for 50 can often be a better performance than 3 for 90.

13. A belief in the importance of wrist-spin in the game to give it balance, variation and entertainment.

THE CAPTAIN'S ROLE

In any team the captain makes the final decision on who will bowl. Thus he has an enormous influence on the success, failure and future of any player. That is a huge responsibility.

Perhaps wrist-spinners have suffered from captaincy more than most. This has been particularly so in the last twenty years, when through a decline in the use of wrist-spin, knowledge of the craft has declined. A generation of captains developed who had not grown up in a wrist-spin age and did not understand the philosophy, tactics or use of wrist-spin. Many bowlers suffered for this ignorance.

Below I set out what I feel is essential knowledge for all captains who may have wrist-spinners in their teams, which is hopefully at every level. Where there are coaches, they too must understand and help their captains where possible.

1. The captain must understand what wrist-spin is about – what the wrist-spinner can do, how he does it, his difficulties, advantages and disadvantages, what he is trying to do. The captain should always be prepared to listen and learn. Don't be too arrogant or stubborn.

2. The captain must be sympathetic to wrist-spin, he must want it, need it. The bowler must feel important, wanted. And that cannot be faked or manufactured. If the captain does not respect and want wrist-spin then either get rid of the wrist-spinner or the captain.

3. A wrist-spinner is an attacking bowler. He must spin the ball hard, which makes it more difficult to attain accuracy, but makes him a more penetrative bowler. To attain the necessary accuracy, he *must* bowl a great deal both in practice and matches.

4. Don't use wrist-spinners as last ditch bowlers, who only go on when everyone else has failed, or two overs before lunch, tea and stumps. All bowlers need to 'build their bowling spell' as a batsman builds his innings. This is even more so of a wrist-spinner

than anyone else, because of the degree of difficulty involved.

5.   Be confident that if you have at your disposal a talented wrist-spinner who is bowling a lot, is confident, knows he is wanted and important in your plan of attack, then you have available a major part of an attack in him alone.

6.   Wrist-spinners are both stock bowlers and strike bowlers.

7.   Wrist-spinners are not automatically inaccurate. Bad wrist-spinners are inaccurate, but so are bad quicks and medium pacers. Good wrist-spinners throughout history have been very accurate indeed.

8.   When the ball is not swinging, medium pacers play batsmen in, particularly new batsmen. New batsmen don't want to have to think. Unless the ball is swinging around, or sometimes even when it is, attack new batsmen with spin.

9.   Down-wind pace and up-wind spin is a highly successful combination.

10.   For the same reasons as in point 8, think of using spinners to open each session of play or to apply pressure in the last hour of play. Open the sessions with bowlers most likely to take a wicket.

11.   Be prepared to use the spinner in an attacking manner whenever the game gets bogged down. Don't accept too easily a game plan of 'contain them, bog them down, and wait for errors'. It is not a successful game plan against good players.

12.   Make the game. Try something different. Always set out to win from the first ball. Don't play safe from the start, then try to win if things go right. Use the motto 'If you think of something attacking and positive, don't wait, do it straight away. If you think of something defensive and negative, don't hurry into it, think it over, it can wait.'
Amidst that kind of positive thinking always have a wrist-spinner (or two) as a key lynchpin.

13.   Talk over field placement with your wrist-spinner. Be sympathetic. Listen. If he is experienced, give him what he wants. If he isn't, be prepared to compromise. Think carefully over field placement to the wrist-spinner. If you are not sure what he is trying to do, find out. Beware bat-pads! They should never be permanent fixtures. It is just as important to loosen batsmen up occasionally, as to tighten them up. Withdrawing the field, to encourage him to play shots, is *aggressive*. Aggressive field placement does not always create aggressive captaincy. Over-use of bat-pad fieldsmen can be negative. A wrist-spinner who spins the ball hard can never be negative and defensive, regardless of the field set. Don't outlaw fieldsmen on the boundary, even two on occasions. Particularly as the bowler settles down.

14.   Understand the importance of wind. Understand the bowler's attitude to line. Understand the importance of drift, drop, bounce, changes

Figs 78–79   The greatest reward for wrist-spinners and wicket-keepers – the
stumping. Tony Greig is deceived by flight and turn, Rod Marsh removes
the bails and Ian Chappell applauds from slip. Three positive, attacking captains
there!

of trajectory, and skid as well as turn. Thus do not impose some hypothetical pace on the bowler.

15. Very few batsmen play good wrist-spin well. This is even more so in the modern game where players are unused to it. *If you have a talented wrist-spinner, he is a valuable possession, but how valuable he eventually is, depends entirely on you.*

16. Don't overuse your quicks. Use them in short spells. If it is not their day, if the conditions are wrong, get them off quickly. If the medium-pacers are not swinging or seaming, don't fall back on containment. Get the wrist-spinners on quickly and attack with them. Or, if you only have one, tie up the down-wind end and attack up-wind with the wrist-spinner – even in the first hour of play.

That should be enough to get a serious captain thinking, so let's look at the clubs and selectors.

THE ROLE OF CLUBS AND SELECTORS

Any club should see itself as part of the overall structure of cricket. Certainly part of its job is to offer enjoyment to cricketers of varying abilities, and to help produce quality teams to compete. But, perhaps more importantly, every club has a duty to set out to identify and develop young players of talent who may be of value in a higher level of cricket.

Such discovery, development and passing on should give pride and pleasure to every club and its members. The success of one of their young products who has been promoted, should rate as highly on the achievement scale as winning a premiership. No clubs, at any level, are worth their salt unless they are heavily involved in the development of youth.

Furthermore, they should understand what qualities are most likely to be wanted and successful at higher levels. They should be encouraging batsmen of the type who are likely to succeed above, not just those who fit the pattern below. The same with bowlers. If the local club can succeed with dribbly medium-pacers who simply bowl tight, short of a length, and wait for the wicket to explode, that should not mean that more penetrative bowling types of greater potential should be discouraged. If a youngster with real pace is discovered, encourage him for his potential, don't trim him to suit the present. If a real wrist-spinner is discovered, encourage him, don't condemn him to 'seam-up' or contain.

The first part of the encouragement process is to make him feel wanted. Encourage him, help him, find good advice for him. Often that means the acceptance that he needs specialist expertise from outside. Then *most importantly* pick him and make sure he is bowled adequately. This means that the club recognizes its responsibilities and appoints selectors who understand and accept them too – selectors who will choose players of potential, and DEMAND that they are used frequently and intelligently enough to develop them. If the appointed captains cannot or will not do that, then the selectors *must* find new captains who will. We cannot simply blame the captain. He has been appointed by the selectors, and the selectors by the club. The ultimate responsibility for what happens on the field rests with the club itself. And an important part of that responsibility, as I have said, is to identify and develop talent which is likely to be valuable at higher levels.

No young bowler is so much at the mercy of clubs, selectors and captains as a wrist-spinner. No matter how much talent he has, no matter how hard he has worked at practice, ultimately his future lies in the hands of these men.

If cricket at the top believes in quality wrist-spin, then those down below must set out to find it and develop it, for it does not simply appear magically at the top from nowhere. It requires a great deal of sympathy, understanding, hard work and regular match play from the earliest stages. As an example, of course, Shane Warne is a wrist-spin product that

Australia, Victoria and the Australian Cricket Academy can be proud of. Their input was immense. But the major credit must go to the following. To the parents, the schools, the clubs, who saw what the boy had to offer at an early age, who nurtured and encouraged it, and carefully passed it along to the higher levels. Shane would never have reached Test cricket – regardless of his enormous ability – unless those people had identified it early, chosen him and allowed him to bowl a great deal.

Clubs, the selectors and captains have the progress and future of their players in their hands. It is a heavy responsibility, and the clear understanding that they are all part of a larger and more important structure is vital.

How each club fares in its league or competition is not the only thing that matters. In the overall pattern of cricket, that is in fact relatively insignificant. But continuing to find and develop youth who may go to the very top, can never be over-emphasized. That duty lies in the hands of all clubs, selectors and captains.

CHAPTER 9

Batting Against Wrist-Spin

As always, your performance against any wrist-spinner will depend greatly on what has taken place long before the actual contest. Over the years, you should have built up an understanding of what the wrist-spinner is trying to do and how he tries to set about it. Part of that is variation of turn, but as I have pointed out in this book, that is only one consideration. Yet it is essential knowledge for a batsman – how the wrist-spinner bowls every possible variation.

This will have required time, interest and work over the years. Reading, talking, watching. The use of nets, matches, television, books, fellow players, coaches and experts. It will demand that you are inquisitive and want to expand your knowledge and experience. You will set out to investigate any new bowler particularly if he is a little different. You will watch him in nets, matches, on television, or video until you know him inside out. You never allow any bowler you come across to avoid such scrutiny. You never become complacent.

All this will demand that you do know how to concentrate totally, that you do, in fact, 'close focus' automatically. If you do not fully understand that, go back to Chapter 5. Now if you have done all this homework – understanding how and why it works,

watching all new bowlers, and ensuring that you do close focus on the ball – you should be confident that you can pick *anything* from the hand. Few bowlers are difficult to pick if you understand, watch carefully and have seen them a few times.

If you come across any bowler in a practice or match situation when you cannot pick everything, or there is any doubt, then you must assume you can pick nothing. This is certainly a disadvantage. Obviously you will have more time and be more able to cash in on a delivery off line or length, if you can pick from the hand and know, in advance, which way it must turn. But, if you cannot pick all, you must assume you can pick none for the time being. Now you should concentrate on watching spin in the air, which often solves the problem. Or speed of footwork can overcome the problem, for he cannot turn, if he cannot bounce. Or you play him off the pitch.

The final resort is to assume that anything outside off-stump on a length will spin in from the off; that anything straight on a length will go on straight, that anything outside leg-stump on a length will turn from the leg. Forward defence covers these, and if it is full or short, you simply hit it. Such tactics sound fine, and they can be. You are 'still in', even though you cannot pick

Fig 80   Abdul Qadir exploding through the crease. Can you pick the wrong'un? Is it the action or the tongue? No, it is the angle of spin in the air. Look at it! (Patrick Eagar)

the bowler, but you do waste so much time and so many runs.

These are the answers if you cannot pick him, but it is far preferable to know which way the ball is going and to see it at once from the hand. I do not believe there is any excuse for an experienced player not to pick everything with confidence from the hand if he works at it intelligently.

So there is your preparation, determined long before the match. What about the match itself? As you build your innings against any spinner,

begin to sort him out. Is he a lesser spinner? That is, one who will offer you a bad ball or two an over? Has he a particularly dangerous ball? Is he a big spinner, a small spinner?

If he is a lesser spinner, then sit on him. Milk him, don't go after him. Take no risks, make sure your defence is tight to his good deliveries, and score off the bad ones, playing the appropriate shots. But if he is a quality spinner, your approach will need to be different. Sitting on him will get you nowhere. He will not bowl regular bad balls, and if you allow him to dominate and bowl how he wants to bowl, it is just a matter of time before he gets you out.

Against the quality spinner, once you have played yourself in, you must go after him, put pressure on him. You cannot allow him to bowl as he wants, you must try to *break up his pattern, and force him to bowl to you.* Now he has to do more than simply settle into a pattern of his choice, he has to work. Quick footwork is one way. Get down the track and hit him on the full. Reduce his margin for error. Pick up the quick singles, particularly if he has bat-pads up, or fieldsmen out. Pressure him. He wants to bowl to one batsman at a time; he certainly does not want batsmen constantly changing ends.

Be prepared to loft into holes, to chip over the top. That does not mean slogging, which will ultimately end in disaster, but simply choosing the right ball, timing it, and preferably hitting straight. Think of changing guard if big turn is concerning you. For instance, if he is bowling around the wicket outside your leg-stump, take guard six inches outside leg-stump. Even more frequent, is big turn pitching on the line of the stumps and leaving you, which can be worrying. Try taking off-stump guard, or even outside off. This is likely to persuade the bowler to change his line of attack to leg-stump or outside leg, when, if you wish, you may re-adjust your guard.

But all of this is aimed at forcing the bowler to rethink, to change his attack, to force him out of his pattern and make him bowl to you. Thus you are taking the initiative. As I have said, you do not need to do this against the poorer spinner, just sit on him and wait. But against the quality spinner, if you are getting bogged down, you should formulate some form of counter-attack. Remember if you can put more pressure on him over a period of time than he can on you, you will usually win the contest.

But wait! Why am I telling all this to batsmen? Why give them any help? After all they are the 'enemy' in a book produced for wrist-spinners. Perhaps the only possible justification

is that at some stage we wrist-spinners, too, must bat. Hopefully, for the future of your career as a wrist-spinner, that will be well up the list as an all-rounder, or at least a more than useful batsman.

And whilst you are at it, make sure you train yourself to be a specialist fieldsman somewhere. It is an immense advantage for a wrist-spinner if he can make himself into a brilliant fieldsman who can bat. In an age, where most teams pick three pace men automatically – and more often than not, they are tailenders – it is a wonderful bonus for the selectors to have a quality spinner who can hold his place at number five, six or seven and be a class fieldsman, particularly a slips catcher. Such a player gives balance to a side, and increases his opportunities of selection and promotion enormously.

Sadly, we cannot expect all selection committees to be dominated by ex-wrist-spinners. Thus we must do all we can with our batting, fielding and bowling to convert the 'heathen'.

CHAPTER 10

The World Spins On

The fair-haired youngster ran up and bowled his leg-spinner. The tennis ball curved nicely, and bounced and turned from the brown mud surface, stamped hard as a rock by countless, bare feet. He jogged up to retrieve it. The pitch set in the centre of the back garden was only twelve yards long, so retrieval and a return to his bowling mark took little time. He bowled again, as he had been doing for the last two hours. As he did most afternoons after school.

Usually brothers or friends were with him and they played a 'Test match'. Serious stuff. But if they were not there, it did not bother him. For he enjoyed it just as much alone with his imagination. For then he became Colin McCool or Bill O'Reilly, imitating the peculiarities of their actions. Bill Johnston and Ernie Toshack were awkward in their left-handedness and Ray Lindwall simply could not fit in to the confines of this small back-yard. But that did not stop him trying.

To the boy, this was not a small back-yard; it was his home ground. The small antiquated outdoor toilet was not a dunny; it was the fieldsman at short mid-wicket. The loquate tree was mid-off. The stairs coming down from the back verandah were leg-slip. And, in his imagination, the ground was surrounded by large ornate grandstands. In fact, the square-leg fence, only ten yards away was a grey paling affair, beyond which stood the neighbour's garage, corrugated iron-roofed. To the boy it was his Members Stand, separated from his majestic ground by a dainty, white painted picket fence.

The only blemish on his ground, as he saw it, was the damned air-raid shelter that Dad had dug between mid-wicket and mid-on. At least it had not encroached onto the wicket area as first envisaged – even wars must be kept in perspective – but it did mar the on-side outfield. He bowled again, then trotted after the ball. It was his fiftieth over today, he calculated. Eight-ball overs, of course.

* * *

It was a beautiful, blue-skied Sydney summer's day and the same boy, six years older, jogged along Sydney Road towards Manly. He was taller, but still slim, pint-sized, blond and tanned. He looked even more so in his white shorts and shirt. He carried a bat over one shoulder; a pair of spiked cricket boots hung from the other. He switched unconsciously from jog to walk and back as he travelled the couple of miles from home to the sea-side suburb of Manly. The final stretch was the steep hill which tumbled down towards the blue of the Pacific and, leaving Sydney Road, he cut through the parks and gardens towards the amphitheatre which was his second home ground, the lovely little Manly Oval.

It was Saturday morning, and he would practice here from 9.00 am, as he had done since he was six. He would bat, carefully watched by Mr Lowe, he would field, then he would bowl, bowl, bowl – hour after hour in the nets. The only interruption would be the ritual icy cold milk-shake – across the tennis courts, over Pittwater Road, to the milk bar. 'Extra milk please! No glass, thanks!' Sucking through the straw straight from the aluminium container, with the occasional drops of perspiration. Bliss!

Then back to the nets to bowl. Sometimes Jimmy Burke came down for a pre-match net, or Alan Walker or Tom Brooks, or, on special occasions, Keith Miller. Heroic figures! Part of the Manly Cricket Club myth and legend. Sometimes he bowled to them.

By mid-day, it was time to go. Off with the spikes, and around the neck with them. Back to bare feet, bat on shoulder, jog up the hill, always so much steeper on the way home. Jog, walk, jog. The few miles of Sydney Road were soon defeated and he rushed into his home, behind which nestled his other home ground – not so frequent a venue now.

Shower and change, sit down to the mix of sandwiches – salad, ham or corned beef – and a cup of tea which his mother never failed to have ready, a quick chat, then it was time to go again. A senior team-mate would pick him up in his car and off they would go to the cricket match somewhere around Sydney for a 2.00 pm start.

That was his Saturday, every summer Saturday he could remember. It began setting off for cricket about 8.00 am and ended when he returned about 8.00 pm. That was his life. It always had been! What else could there possibly be?

*   *   *

The coach watched the two boys with interest and spoke to them with enthusiasm. They were young leg-spinners, good lads it seemed, keen and talented. He spoke to them as he had to so many thousands of youngsters over the last thirty years. Now it was 1994, fifty years since his own youthful experimentation in the backyard.

And here he was at Rossal School, up on the coast of North-West Lancashire next to the Irish Sea and all its gale force wind, speaking to two young Australian bowlers making their first schoolboy cricket tour of England. He watched them with more than a little nostalgia. One of them, in particular, looked good. He was rhythmical, he spun the ball hard, and it came out well. He knew what he was trying to do and understood most of the variations though, not surprisingly, he did not yet have adequate control. He came up to offer thanks to the coach for the hour's help he had given him. The coach regarded him carefully catching his eyes,

'Do you like leg-spinning, Trent?' he asked, using that same carefully chosen question he had asked so many others so often before.

Fig 81.

'Very much, Mr Philpott', he replied.

'But do you love it, son?' said the coach.

The boy looked back thoughtfully, trying to come fully to grips with the question. He was relaxed, quite open, the young clean cut face quite unblemished, and once again the coach marvelled at the beauty and innocence of a teenage boy when he is doing what he wants to do.

At last, he smiled, and spoke, 'Yes, I really do love it, Mr Philpott. I think that being a successful wrist-spin bowler means more to me than any other single thing in life.'

The coach nodded, for that was the answer he had expected, and the two of them communicated with the understanding smiles of acknowledged fellow travellers.

*   *   *

Life goes on. Little changes. Amidst the inevitable disappointments, the world can be a wonderful place.

Whilst it continues to spin, that is!

Index